Sādhanā

The Realisation of Life

MAVEN BOOKS

Sādhanā

The Realisation of Life

Rabindranath Tagore

MAVEN BOOKS

Chennai Trichy Tirunelveli New Delhi

MAVEN BOOKS

An Imprint of **MJP Publishers**

ISBN 978-93-87488-06-9

Maven Books
No. 44, Nallathambi Street,
Triplicane, Chennai 600 005

MJP 384

Publisher : **C. Janarthanan**

Publisher's Note

The legacy of a country is in its varied cultural heritage, historical literature, developments in the field of economy and science. The top nations in the world are competing in the field of science, economy and literature. This vast legacy has to be conserved and documented so that it can be bestowed to the future generation. The knowledge of this legacy is slowly getting perished in the present generation due to lack of documentation.

Keeping this in mind, the concern with retrospective acquiring of rare books has been accented recently by the burgeoning reprint industry. Maven Books is gratified to retrieve the rare collections with a view to bring back those books that were landmarks in their time.

In this effort, a series of rare books would be republished under the banner, "Maven Books". The books in the reprint series have been carefully selected for their contemporary usefulness as well as their historical importance within the intellectual. We reconstruct the book with slight enhancements made for better presentation, without affecting the contents of the original edition.

Most of the works selected for republishing covers a huge range of subjects, from history to anthropology. We believe this reprint edition will be a service to the numerous researchers and practitioners active in this fascinating field. We allow readers to experience the wonder of peering into a scholarly work of the highest order and seminal significance.

Maven Books

Preface

Perhaps it is well for me to explain that the subject-matter of the papers published in this book has not been philosophically treated, nor has it been approached from the scholar's point of view. The writer has been brought up in a family where texts of the Upanishads are used in daily worship; and he has had before him the example of his father, who lived his long life in the closest communion with God, while not neglecting his duties to the world, or allowing his keen interest in all human affairs to suffer any abatement. So in these papers, it may be hoped, western readers will have an opportunity of coming into touch with the ancient spirit of India as revealed in our sacred texts and manifested in the life of to-day.

All the great utterances of man have to be judged not by the letter but by the spirit—the spirit which unfolds itself with the growth of life in history. We get to know the real meaning of Christianity by observing its living aspect at the present moment—however different that may be, even in important respects, from the Christianity of earlier periods.

For western scholars the great religious scriptures of India seem to possess merely a retrospective and archælogical interest; but to us they are of living importance, and we cannot help thinking that they lose their significance when exhibited in labelled cases—mummied specimens of human thought and aspiration, preserved for all time in the wrappings of erudition.

The meaning of the living words that come out of the experiences of great hearts can never be exhausted by any one system of logical interpretation. They have to be endlessly explained by the commentaries of individual lives, and they gain an added mystery in each new revelation. To me the verses of the Upanishads and the teachings of Buddha have ever been things of the spirit, and therefore endowed with boundless vital growth; and I have used them, both in my own life and in my preaching, as being instinct with individual meaning for me, as for others, and awaiting for their confirmation, my own special testimony, which must have its value because of its individuality.

I should add perhaps that these papers embody in a connected form, suited to this publication, ideas which have been culled from several of the Bengali discourses which I am in the habit of giving to my students in my school at Bolpur in Bengal; and I have used here and there translations of passages from these done by my friends, Babu Satish Chandra Roy and Babu Ajit Kumar Chakravarti. The last paper of this series, "Realisation in Action," has been translated from my Bengali discourse on "Karma-yoga" by my nephew, Babu Surendra Nath Tagore.

I take this opportunity of expressing my gratitude to Professor James H. Woods, of Harvard University, for his generous appreciation which encouraged me to complete this series of papers and read most of them before the Harvard University. And I offer my thanks to Mr. Ernest Rhys for his kindness in helping me with suggestions and revisions, and in going through the proofs.

A word may be added about the pronouncing of Sādhanā: the accent falls decisively on the first ā, which has the broad sound of the letter.

Contents

I.	The Relation of the Individual to the Universe	1
II.	Soul Consciousness	17
III.	The Problem of Evil	33
IV.	The Problem of Self	47
V.	Realisation in Love	65
VI.	Realisation in Action	83
VII.	The Realisation of Beauty	95
VIII.	The Realisation of the Infinite	101

I

THE RELATION OF THE INDIVIDUAL TO THE UNIVERSE

The civilisation of ancient Greece was nurtured within city walls. In fact, all the modern civilisations have their cradles of brick and mortar.

These walls leave their mark deep in the minds of men. They set up a principle of "divide and rule" in our mental outlook, which begets in us a habit of securing all our conquests by fortifying them and separating them from one another. We divide nation and nation, knowledge and knowledge, man and nature. It breeds in us a strong suspicion of whatever is beyond the barriers we have built, and everything has to fight hard for its entrance into our recognition.

When the first Aryan invaders appeared in India it was a vast land of forests, and the new-comers rapidly took advantage of them. These forests afforded them shelter from the fierce heat of the sun and the ravages of tropical storms, pastures for cattle, fuel for sacrificial fire, and materials for building cottages. And the different Aryan clans with their patriarchal heads settled in the different forest tracts which had some special advantage of natural protection, and food and water in plenty.

Thus in India it was in the forests that our civilisation had its birth, and it took a distinct character from this origin and environment. It was surrounded by the vast life of nature, was fed and clothed by her, and had the closest and most constant intercourse with her varying aspects.

Such a life, it may be thought, tends to have the effect of dulling human intelligence and dwarfing the incentives to progress by lowering the standards of existence. But in ancient India we find that the circumstances of forest life did not overcome man's mind, and did not enfeeble the current of his energies, but only gave to it a particular direction. Having been in constant contact with the living growth of nature, his mind was free from the desire to extend his dominion by erecting boundary walls around his acquisitions. His aim was not to acquire but to realise, to enlarge his consciousness by growing with and growing into his surroundings. He felt that truth is all-comprehensive, that there is no such thing as absolute isolation in existence, and the only way of attaining truth is through the interpenetration of our being into all objects. To realise this great harmony between man's spirit and the spirit of the world was the endeavour of the forest-dwelling sages of ancient India.

In later days there came a time when these primeval forests gave way to cultivated fields, and wealthy cities sprang up on all sides. Mighty kingdoms were established, which had communications with all the great powers of the world. But even in the heyday of its material prosperity the heart of India ever looked back with adoration upon the early ideal of strenuous self-realisation, and the dignity of the simple life of the forest hermitage, and drew its best inspiration from the wisdom stored there.

The west seems to take a pride in thinking that it is subduing nature; as if we are living in a hostile world where we have to wrest everything we want from an unwilling and alien arrangement of things. This sentiment is the product of the city-wall habit and training of mind. For in the city life man naturally directs the concentrated light of his mental vision upon his own life and works, and this creates an artificial dissociation between himself and the Universal Nature within whose bosom he lies.

But in India the point of view was different; it included the world with the man as one great truth. India put all her emphasis on the harmony that exists between the individual and the universal. She felt we could have no communication whatever with our surroundings if they were absolutely foreign to us. Man's complaint against nature is that he has to acquire most of his necessaries by his own efforts. Yes, but his efforts are not in vain; he is reaping success every day, and that shows there is a rational connection between him and nature, for we never can make anything our own except that which is truly related to us.

We can look upon a road from two different points of view. One regards it as dividing us from the object of our desire; in that case we count every step of our journey over it as something attained by force in the face of obstruction. The other sees it as the road which leads us to our destination; and as such it is part of our goal. It is already the beginning of our attainment, and by journeying over it we can only gain that which in itself it offers to us. This last point of view is that of India with regard to nature. For her, the great fact is that we are in harmony with nature; that man can think because his thoughts are in harmony with things; that he can use the forces of nature for his own purpose only because his power is in harmony with the power which is universal, and that in the long run his purpose never can knock against the purpose which works through nature.

In the west the prevalent feeling is that nature belongs exclusively to inanimate things and to beasts, that there is a sudden unaccountable break where human-nature begins. According to it, everything that is low in the scale of beings is merely nature, and whatever has the stamp of perfection on it, intellectual or moral, is human-nature. It is like dividing the bud and the blossom into two separate categories, and putting their grace to the credit of two different and antithetical principles. But the Indian mind never has any hesitation in acknowledging its kinship with nature, its unbroken relation with all.

The fundamental unity of creation was not simply a philosophical speculation for India; it was her life-object to realise this great harmony in feeling and in action. With mediation and service, with a regulation of life, she cultivated her consciousness in such a way that everything had a spiritual meaning to her. The earth, water and light, fruits and flowers, to her were not merely physical phenomena to be turned to use and then left aside. They were necessary to her in the attainment of her ideal of perfection, as every note is necessary to the completeness of the symphony. India intuitively felt that the essential fact of this world has a vital meaning for us; we have to be fully alive to it and establish a conscious relation with it, not merely impelled by scientific curiosity or greed of material advantage, but realising it in the spirit of sympathy, with a large feeling of joy and peace.

The man of science knows, in one aspect, that the world is not merely what it appears to be to our senses; he knows that earth and water are really the play of forces that manifest themselves to us as earth and water–how, we can but partially apprehend. Likewise the man who has his spiritual eyes open knows that the ultimate truth about earth and water lies in our apprehension of the eternal will which works in time and takes shape in the forces we realise under those aspects. This is not mere knowledge, as science is, but it is a preception of the soul by the soul. This does not lead us to power, as knowledge does, but it gives us joy, which is the product of the union of kindred things. The man whose acquaintance with the world does not lead him deeper than science leads him, will never understand what it is that the man with the spiritual vision finds in these natural phenomena. The water does not merely cleanse his limbs, but it purifies his heart; for it touches his soul. The earth does not merely hold his body, but it gladdens his mind; for its contact is more than a physical contact–it is a living presence. When a man does not realise his kinship with the world, he lives in a prison-house whose walls are alien to him. When he meets the eternal spirit in all objects, then is he emancipated, for then he discovers the fullest significance of the world into which he is born; then he finds himself in perfect truth, and his harmony with the all is established. In India men are enjoined to be fully awake to the fact that they are in the closest relation to things around them, body and soul, and that they are to hail the morning sun, the flowing water, the fruitful earth, as the manifestation of the same living truth which holds them in its embrace. Thus the text of our everyday meditation is the *Gayathri*, a verse which is considered to be the epitome of all the Vedas. By its help we try to realise the essential unity of the world with the conscious soul of man; we learn to perceive the unity held together by the one Eternal Spirit, whose power creates the earth, the sky, and the stars, and at the same time irradiates our minds with the light of a consciousness that moves and exists in unbroken continuity with the outer world.

It is not true that India has tried to ignore differences of value in different things, for she knows that would make life impossible. The sense of the superiority of man in the scale of creation has not been absent from her mind. But she has had her own idea as to that in which his superiority really consists. It is not in the power of possession but in the power of union. Therefore India chose her places of pilgrimage wherever there was in nature some special grandeur or beauty, so that her mind could come out of its world of narrow necessities and realise its place in the infinite. This was the reason why in India a whole people who once were meat-eaters gave up taking animal food to cultivate the sentiment of universal sympathy for life, an event unique in the history of mankind.

India knew that when by physical and mental barriers we violently detach ourselves from the inexhaustible life of nature; when we become merely man, but not man-in-the-universe, we create bewildering problems, and having shut off the source of their solution, we try all kinds of artificial methods each of which brings its own crop of interminable difficulties. When man leaves his resting-place in universal nature, when he walks on the single rope of humanity, it means either a dance or a fall for him, he has ceaselessly to strain every nerve and muscle to keep his balance at each step, and then, in the intervals of his weariness, he fulminates against Providence and feels a secret pride and satisfaction in thinking that he has been unfairly dealt with by the whole scheme of things.

But this cannot go on for ever. Man must realise the wholeness of his existence, his place in the infinite; he must know that hard as he may strive he can never create his honey within the cells of his hive; for the perennial supply of his life food is outside their walls. He must know that when man shuts himself out from the vitalising and purifying touch of the infinite, and falls back upon himself for his sustenance and his healing, then he goads himself into madness, tears himself into shreds, and eats his own substance. Deprived of the background of the whole, his poverty loses its one great quality, which is simplicity, and becomes squalid and shamefaced. His wealth is no longer magnanimous; it grows merely extravagant. His appetites do not minister to his life, keeping to the limits of their purpose; they become an end in themselves and set fire to his life and play the fiddle in the lurid light of the conflagration. Then it is that in our self-expression we try to startle and not to attract; in art we strive for originality and lose sight of truth which is old and yet ever new; in literature we miss the complete view of man which is simple and yet great, but he appears as a psychological problem or the embodiment of a passion that is intense because abnormal and because exhibited in the glare of a fiercely emphatic light which is artificial. When man's consciousness is restricted only to the immediate vicinity of his human self, the deeper roots of his nature do not find their permanent soil, his spirit is ever on the brink of starvation, and in the place of healthful strength he substitutes rounds of stimulation. Then it is that man misses his inner perspective and measures his greatness by its bulk and not by its vital link with the infinite, judges his activity by its movement and not by the repose of perfection–the repose which is in the starry heavens, in the ever-flowing rhythmic dance of creation.

The first invasion of India has its exact parallel in the invasion of America by the European settlers. They also were confronted with primeval forests and a fierce struggle with aboriginal races. But this struggle between man and man, and man and nature lasted till the very end; they never came to any terms. In India the forests which were the habitation of the barbarians became the sanctuary of sages, but in America these great living cathedrals of nature had no deeper significance to man. The brought wealth and power to him, and perhaps at times they ministered to his enjoyment of beauty, and inspired a solitary poet. They never acquired a sacred association in the hearts of men as the site of some great spiritual reconcilement where man's soul has its meeting-place with the soul of the world.

I do not for a moment wish to suggest that these things should have been otherwise. It would be an utter waste of opportunities if history were to repeat itself exactly in the same manner in every place. It is best for the commerce of the spirit that people differently situated should bring their different products into the market of humanity, each of which is complementary and necessary to the others. All that I wish to say is that India at the outset of her career met with a special combination of circumstances which was not lost upon her. She had, according to her opportunities, thought and pondered, striven and suffered, dived into the depths of existence, and achieved something which surely cannot be without its value to people whose evolution in history took a different way altogether. Man for his perfect growth requires all the living elements that constitute his complex life; that is why his food has to be cultivated in different fields and brought from different sources.

Civilisation is a kind of mould that each nation is busy making for itself to shape its men and women according to its best ideal. All its institutions, its legislature, its standard of approbation and condemnation, its conscious and unconscious teachings tend toward that object. The modern civilisation of the west, by all its organised efforts, is trying to turn out men perfect in physical, intellectual, and moral efficiency. There the vast energies of the nations are employed in extending man's power over his surroundings, and people are combining and straining every faculty to possess and to turn to account all that they can lay their hands upon, to overcome every obstacle on their path of conquest. They are ever disciplining themselves to fight nature and other races; their armaments are getting more and more stupendous every day; their machines, their appliances, their organisations go on multiplying at an amazing rate. This is a splendid achievement, no doubt, and a wonderful manifestation of man's masterfulness which knows no obstacle, and which has for its object the supremacy of himself over everything else.

The ancient civilisation of India had its own ideal of perfection towards which its efforts were directed. Its aim was not attaining power, and it neglected to cultivate to the utmost its capacities, and to organise men for defensive and offensive purposes, for co-operation in the acquisition of wealth and for military and political ascendancy. The ideal that India tried to realise led her best men to the isolation of a contemplative life, and the treasures that she gained for mankind by penetrating into the mysteries of reality cost her dear in the sphere of worldly success. Yet, this also was a sublime achievement,–it was a supreme manifestation of that human aspiration which knows no limit, and which has for its object nothing less than the realisation of the Infinite.

There were the virtuous, the wise, the courageous; there were the statesmen, kings and emperors of India; but whom amongst all these classes did she look up to and choose to be the representative of men?

They were the rishis. What were the rishis? *They who having attained the supreme soul in knowledge were filled with wisdom, and having found him in union with the soul were in perfect harmony with the inner self; they having realised him in the heart were free from all selfish desires, and having experienced him in all the activities of the world, had attained calmness. The rishis were they who having reached the supreme God from all sides had found abiding peace, had become united with all, had entered into the life of the Universe*[1].

Thus the state of realising our relationship with all, of entering into everything through union with God, was considered in India to be the ultimate end and fulfilment of humanity.

Man can destroy and plunder, earn and accumulate, invent and discover, but he is great because his soul comprehends all. It is dire destruction for him when he envelopes his

1. Samprāpyainam rishayo jñānatripatāh Kritātmānō vītarāgāh praçantāh tē sarvagam sarvatah prāpya dhīrāh Yuktātmānah sarvamēvāviçanti.

soul in a dead shell of callous habits, and when a blind fury of works whirls round him like an eddying dust storm, shutting out the horizon. That indeed kills the very spirit of his being, which is the spirit of comprehension. Essentially man is not a slave either of himself or of the world; but he is a lover. His freedom and fulfilment is in love, which is another name for perfect comprehension. By this power of comprehension, this permeation of his being, he is united with the all-pervading Spirit, who is also the breath of his soul. Where a man tries to raise himself to eminence by pushing and jostling all others, to achieve a distinction by which he prides himself to be more than everybody else, there he is alienated from that Spirit. This is why the Upanishads describe those who have attained the goal of human life as "*peaceful*"[2] and as "*at-one-with-God,*"[3] meaning that they are in perfect harmony with man and nature, and therefore in undisturbed union with God.

We have a glimpse of the same truth in the teachings of Jesus when he says, "It is easier for a camel to pass through the eye of a needle than for a rich man to enter the kingdom of Heaven"–which implies that whatever we treasure for ourselves separates us from others; our possessions are our limitations. He who is bent upon accumulating riches is unable, with his ego continually bulging, to pass through the gates of comprehension of the spiritual world, which is the world of perfect harmony; he is shut up within the narrow walls of his limited acquisitions.

Hence the spirit of the teachings of Upanishad is: In order to find him you must embrace all. In the pursuit of wealth you really give up everything to gain a few things, and that is not the way to attain him who is completeness.

---

2. Praçantāh
3. Yuktātmānah

Some modern philosophers of Europe, who are directly or indirectly indebted to the Upanishads, far from realising their debt, maintain that the Brahma of India is a mere abstraction, a negation of all that is in the world. In a word, that the Infinite Being is to be found nowhere except in metaphysics. It may be, that such a doctrine has been and still is prevalent with a section of our countrymen. But this is certainly not in accord with the pervading spirit of the Indian mind. Instead, it is the practice of realising and affirming the presence of the infinite in all things which has been its constant inspiration.

We are enjoined to see *whatever there is in the world as being enveloped by God.*[4]

I bow to God over and over again who is in fire and in water, who permeates the whole world, who is in the annual crops as well as in the perennial trees.[5]

Can this be God abstracted from the world? Instead, it signifies not merely seeing him in all things, but saluting him in all the objects of the world. The attitude of the God-conscious man of the Upanishad towards the universe is one of a deep feeling of adoration. His object of worship is present everywhere. It is the one living truth that makes all realities true. This truth is not only of knowledge but of devotion. '*Namonamah,*'– we bow to him everywhere, and over and over again. It is recognised in the outburst of the Rishi, who addresses the whole world in a sudden ecstasy of joy: *Listen to me, ye sons of the immortal spirit, ye who live in the heavenly abode, I have known the Supreme Person whose light shines forth from beyond the darkness.*[6] Do we not find the overwhelming delight of a direct

4. Içāvāsyamidam sarvam yat kiñcha jagatyāñ jagat.
5. Yo dēvō'gnau y'ōpsu y'ō viçvambhuvanamāvivēça ya ōshadhishu yō vanaspatishu tasmai dēvāya namōnamah.
6. Çrinvantu viçve amritasya putrā ā ye divya dhāmāni tasthuh vedāhametam purusham mahāntam āditya varṇam tamasah parastāt.

and positive experience where there is not the least trace of vagueness or passivity?

Buddha who developed the practical side of the teaching of Upanishads, preached the same message when he said, *With everything, whether it is above or below, remote or near, visible or invisible, thou shalt preserve a relation of unlimited love without any animosity or without a desire to kill. To live in such a consciousness while standing or walking, sitting or lying down till you are asleep, is Brahma vihāra, or, in other words, is living and moving and having your joy in the spirit of Brahma.*

What is that spirit? The Upanishad says, *The being who is in his essence the light and life of all, who is world-conscious, is Brahma.*[7] To feel all, to be conscious of everything, is his spirit. We are immersed in his consciousness body and soul. It is through his consciousness that the sun attracts the earth; it is through his consciousness that the light-waves are being transmitted from planet to planet.

Not only in space, but *this light and life, this all-feeling being is in our souls.*[8] He is all-conscious in space, or the world of extension; and he is all-conscious in soul, or the world of intension.

Thus to attain our world-consciousness, we have to unite our feeling with this all-pervasive infinite feeling. In fact, the only true human progress is coincident with this widening of the range of feeling. All our poetry, philosophy, science, art and religion are serving to extend the scope of our consciousness towards higher and larger spheres. Man does not acquire rights through occupation of larger space, nor through external conduct, but his rights extend only so far as he is real, and his reality is measured by the scope of his consciousness.

7. Yaçchāyamasminnākāçē tējōmayō'mritamayah purushah sarvānubhūh.
8. Yaçchāyamasminnātmani tējōmayō'mritamayah purushah sarvānubhūh.

We have, however, to pay a price for this attainment of the freedom of consciousness. What is the price? It is to give one's self away. Our soul can realise itself truly only by denying itself. The Upanishad says, *Thou shalt gain by giving away*[9], *Thou shalt not covet.*[10]

In Gita we are advised to work disinterestedly, abandoning all lust for the result. Many outsiders conclude from this teaching that the conception of the world as something unreal lies at the root of the so-called disinterestedness preached in India. But the reverse is true.

The man who aims at his own aggrandisement underrates everything else. Compared to his ego the rest of the world is unreal. Thus in order to be fully conscious of the reality of all, one has to be free himself from the bonds of personal desires. This discipline we have to go through to prepare ourselves for our social duties—for sharing the burdens of our fellow-beings. Every endeavour to attain a larger life requires of man "to gain by giving away, and not to be greedy." And thus to expand gradually the consciousness of one's unity with all is the striving of humanity.

The Infinite in India was not a thin nonentity, void of all content. The Rishis of India asserted emphatically, "To know him in this life is to be true; not to know him in this life is the desolation of death."[11] How to know him then? "By realising him in each and all."[12] Not only in nature but in the family, in society, and in the state, the more we realise the World-conscious in all, the better for us. Failing to realise it, we turn our faces to destruction.

---

9. Tyaktēna bhuñjīthāh
10. Mā gridhah
11. Iha chēt avēdit atha satyamasti, nachēt iha avēdit mahatī vinashtih.
12. Bhūtēshu bhūtēshu vichintva.

It fills me with great joy and a high hope for the future of humanity when I realise that there was a time in the remote past when our poet-prophets stood under the lavish sunshine of an Indian sky and greeted the world with the glad recognition of kindred. It was not an anthropomorphic hallucination. It was not seeing man reflected everywhere in grotesquely exaggerated images, and witnessing the human drama acted on a gigantic scale in nature's arena of flitting lights and shadows. On the contrary, it meant crossing the limiting barriers of the individual, to become more than man, to become one with the All. It was not a mere play of the imagination, but it was the liberation of consciousness from all the mystifications and exaggerations of the self. These ancient seers felt in the serene depth of their mind that the same energy which vibrates and passes into the endless forms of the world manifests itself in our inner being as consciousness; and there is no break in unity. For these seers there was no gap in their luminous vision of perfection. They never acknowledged even death itself as creating a chasm in the field of reality. They said, *His reflection is death as well as immortality*[13]. They did not recognise any essential opposition between life and death, and they said with absolute assurance, "It is life that is death."[14] They saluted with the same serenity of gladness "life in its aspect of appearing and in its aspect of departure"—*That which is past is hidden in life, and that which is to come.*[15] They knew that mere appearance and disappearance are on the surface like waves on the sea, but life which is permanent knows no decay or diminution.

Everything has sprung from immortal life and is vibrating with life,[16] *for life is immense.*[17]

13. Yasya chhāyāmritam yasya mrityuh.
14. Prāno mrityuh.
15. Namō astu āyatē namō astu parāyatē. Prānē ha bhūtam bhavyañcha.
16. Yadidan kiñcha praṇa ejati nihsritam.
17. Prāno virāt.

This is the noble heritage from our forefathers waiting to be claimed by us as our own, this ideal of the supreme freedom of consciousness. It is not merely intellectual or emotional, it has an ethical basis, and it must be translated into action. In the Upanishad it is said, *The supreme being is all-pervading, therefore he is the innate good in all.*[18] To be truly united in knowledge, love, and service with all beings, and thus to realise one's self in the all-pervading God is the essence of goodness, and this is the keynote of the teachings of the Upanishads: *Life is immense!*[19]

18. Sarvavyāpī sa bhagavān tasmāt sarvagatah çivah.

19. Prāṇo virāt.

II

SOUL CONSCIOUSNESS

We have seen that it was the aspiration of ancient India to live and move and have its joy in Brahma, the all-conscious and all-pervading Spirit, by extending its field of consciousness over all the world. But that, it may be urged, is an impossible task for man to achieve. If this extension of consciousness be an outward process, then it is endless; it is like attempting to cross the ocean after ladling out its water. By beginning to try to realise all, one has to end by realising nothing.

But, in reality, it is not so absurd as it sounds. Man has every day to solve this problem of enlarging his region and adjusting his burdens. His burdens are many, too numerous for him to carry, but he knows that by adopting a system he can lighten the weight of his load. Whenever they feel too complicated and unwieldy, he knows it is because he has not been able to hit upon the system which would have set everything in place and distributed the weight evenly. This search for system is really a search for unity, for synthesis; it is our attempt to harmonise the heterogeneous complexity of outward materials by an inner adjustment. In the search we gradually become aware that to find out the One is to possess the All; that there, indeed, is our last and highest privilege. It is based on the law of that unity which is, if we only know it, our abiding strength. Its living principle is the power that is in truth; the truth of that unity which comprehends multiplicity. Facts are many, but the truth is one. The animal intelligence knows facts, the human mind has power to apprehend truth. The apple falls from the tree, the rain descends upon the earth–you can go on burdening your memory with such facts and never come to an end. But once you get hold of the law of gravitation you can dispense with the necessity of collecting facts *ad infinitum*. You have got at one truth which governs numberless facts. This discovery of truth is pure joy to man–it is a liberation of his mind. For, a mere fact is like a blind lane, it leads only to itself–it has no beyond. But a truth opens up a whole horizon, it leads us to the infinite. That is the reason why, when a man like Darwin discovers some simple general truth about Biology, it does not stop there, but like a lamp shedding its light far beyond the object for which it was lighted, it illumines the whole region of human life and thought, transcending its original purpose. Thus we find that truth, while investing all facts, is not a mere aggregate of facts–it surpasses them on all sides and points to the infinite reality.

As in the region of knowledge so in that of consciousness, man must clearly realise some central truth which will give him an outlook over the widest possible field. And that is the object which the Upanishad has in view when it says, *Know thine own Soul*. Or, in other words, realise the one great principal of unity that there is in every man.

All our egoistic impulses, our selfish desires, obscure our true vision of the soul. For they only indicate our own narrow self. When we are conscious of our soul, we perceive the inner being that transcends our ego and has its deeper affinity with the All.

Children, when they begin to learn each separate letter of the alphabet, find no pleasure in it, because they miss the real purpose of the lesson; in fact, while letters claim our attention only in themselves and as isolated things, they fatigue us. They become a source of joy to us only when they combine into words and sentences and convey an idea.

Likewise, our soul when detached and imprisoned within the narrow limits of a self loses its significance. For its very essence is unity. It can only find out its truth by unifying itself with others, and only then it has its joy. Man was troubled and he lived in a state of fear so long as he had not discovered the uniformity of law in nature; till then the world was alien to him. The law that he discovered is nothing but the perception of harmony that prevails between reason which is of the soul of man and the workings of the world. This is the bond of union through which man is related to the world in which he lives, and he feels an exceeding joy when he finds this out, for then he realises himself in his surroundings. To understand anything is to find in it something which is our own, and it is the discovery of ourselves outside us which makes us glad. This relation of understanding is partial, but the relation of love is complete. In love the sense of difference is obliterated and the human soul fulfils its purpose in perfection, transcending the limits of itself and reaching across the threshold of the infinite. Therefore love is the highest bliss that man can attain to, for through it alone he truly knows that he is more than himself, and that he is at one with the All.

This principal of unity which man has in his soul is ever active, establishing relations far and wide through literature, art, and science, society, statecraft, and religion. Our great Revealers are they who make manifest the true meaning of the soul by giving up self for the love of mankind. They face calumny and persecution, deprivation and death in their service of love. They live the life of the soul, not of the self, and thus they prove to us the ultimate truth of humanity. We call them *Mahātmās*, "the men of the great soul."

It is said in one of the Upanishads: *It is not that thou lovest thy son because thou desirest him, but thou lovest thy son because thou desirest thine own soul.*[20] The meaning of this is, that whomsoever we love, in him we find our own soul in the highest sense. The final truth of our existence lies in this. *Paramātmā*, the supreme soul, is in me, as well as in my son, and my joy in my son is the realisation of this truth. It has become quite a commonplace fact, yet it is wonderful to think upon, that the joys and sorrows of our loved ones are joys and sorrows to us—nay they are more. Why so? Because in them we have grown larger, in them we have touched that great truth which comprehends the whole universe.

It very often happens that our love for our children, our friends, or other loved ones, debars us from the further realisation of our soul. It enlarges our scope of consciousness, no doubt, yet it sets a limit to its freest expansion. Nevertheless, it is the first step, and all the wonder lies in this first step itself. It shows to us the true nature of our soul. From it we know, for certain, that our highest joy is in the losing of our egoistic self and in the uniting with others. This love gives us a new power and insight and beauty of mind to the extent of the limits we set around it, but ceases to do so if those limits lose their elasticity, and militate against the spirit of love altogether; then our friendships become exclusive, our families selfish and inhospitable, our nations insular and aggressively inimical to other races. It is like putting a burning light within a sealed enclosure, which shines brightly till the poisonous gases accumulate and smother the flame. Nevertheless it has proved its truth before it dies, and made known the joy of freedom from the grip of darkness, blind and empty and cold.

According to the Upanishads, the key to cosmic consciousness, to God-consciousness, is in the consciousness of

20. Na vā arē putrasya kāmāya putraḥ priyō bhavati, ātmanastu kāmāya putraḥ priyō bhavati.

the soul. To know our soul apart from the self is the first step towards the realisation of the supreme deliverance. We must know with absolute certainty that essentially we are spirit. This we can do by winning mastery over self, by rising above all pride and greed and fear, by knowing that worldly losses and physical death can take nothing away from the truth and the greatness of our soul. The chick knows when it breaks through the self-centered isolation of its egg that the hard shell which covered it so long was not really a part of its life. That shell is a dead thing, it has no growth, it affords no glimpse whatever of the vast beyond that lies outside it. However pleasantly perfect and rounded it may be, it must be given a blow to, it must be burst through and thereby the freedom of light and air be won, and the complete purpose of bird life be achieved. In Sanskrit, the bird has been called the twice-born. So too the man who has gone through the ceremony of the discipline of self-restraint and high thinking for a period of at least twelve years; who has come out simple in wants, pure in heart, and ready to take up all the responsibilities of life in a disinterested largeness of spirit. He is considered to have had his rebirth from the blind envelopment of self to the freedom of soul life; to have come into living relation with his surroundings; to have become at one with the All.

I have already warned my hearers, and must once more warn them against the idea that the teachers of India preached a renunciation of the world and of self which leads only to the blank emptiness of negation. Their aim was the realisation of the soul, or, in other words, gaining the world in perfect truth. When Jesus said, "Blessed are the meek, for they shall inherit the earth," he meant this. He proclaimed the truth that when man gets rid of his pride of self then he comes into his true inheritance. No more has he to fight his way into his position in the world; it is secure for him everywhere by the immortal right of his soul. Pride of self interferes with the proper function of the soul which is to realise itself by perfecting its union with the world and the world's God.

In his sermon to Sádhu Simha Buddha says, *It is true, Simha, that I denounce activities, but only the activities that lead to the evil in words, thoughts, or deeds. It is true, Simha, that I preach extinction, but only the extinction of pride, lust, evil thought, and ignorance, not that of forgiveness, love, charity, and truth.*

The doctrine of deliverance that Buddha preached was the freedom from the thraldom of *Avidyā*. *Avidyā* is the ignorance that darkens our consciousness, and tends to limit it within the boundaries of our personal self. It is this *Avidyā*, this ignorance, this limiting of consciousness that creates the hard separateness of the ego, and thus becomes the source of all pride and greed and cruelty incidental to self-seeking. When a man sleeps he is shut up within the narrow activities of his physical life. He lives, but he knows not the varied relations of his life to his surroundings,–therefore he knows not himself. So when a man lives the life of *Avidyā* he is confined within his self. It is a spiritual sleep; his consciousness is not fully awake to the highest reality that surrounds him, therefore he knows not the reality of his own soul. When he attains *Bodhi*, i.e. the awakenment from the sleep of self to the perfection of consciousness, he becomes Buddha.

Once I met two ascetics of a certain religious sect in a village of Bengal. "Can you tell me," I asked them, "wherein lies the special features of your religion?" One of them hesitated for a moment and answered, "It is difficult to define that." The other said, "No, it is quite simple. We hold that we have first of all to know our own soul under the guidance of our spiritual teacher, and when we have done that we can find him, who is the Supreme Soul, within us." "Why don't you preach your doctrine to all the people of the world?" I asked. "Whoever feels thirsty will of himself come to the river," was his reply. "But then, do you find it so? Are they coming?" The man gave a gentle smile, and with an assurance which had not the least tinge of impatience or anxiety, he said, "They must come, one and all."

Yes, he is right, this simple ascetic of rural Bengal. Man is indeed abroad to satisfy needs which are more to him than food and clothing. He is out to find himself. Man's history is the history of his journey to the unknown in quest of the realisation of his immortal self–his soul. Through the rise and fall of empires; through the building up gigantic piles of wealth and the ruthless scattering of them upon the dust; through the creation of vast bodies of symbols that give shape to his dreams and aspirations, and the casting of them away like the playthings of an outworn infancy; through his forging of magic keys with which to unlock the mysteries of creation, and through his throwing away of this labour of ages to go back to his workshop and work up afresh some new form; yes, through it all man is marching from epoch to epoch towards the fullest realisation of his soul,–the soul which is greater than the things man accumulates, the deeds he accomplishes, the theories he builds; the soul whose onward course is never checked by death or dissolution. Man's mistakes and failures have by no means been trifling or small, they have strewn his path with colossal ruins; his sufferings have been immense, like birth-pangs for a giant child; they are the prelude of a fulfilment whose scope is infinite. Man has gone through and is still undergoing martyrdoms in various ways, and his institutions are the altars he has built whereto he brings his daily sacrifices, marvellous in kind and stupendous in quantity. All this would be absolutely unmeaning and unbearable if all along he did not feel that deepest joy of the soul within him, which tries its divine strength by suffering and proves its exhaustless riches by renunciation. Yes, they are coming, the pilgrims, one and all–coming to their true inheritance of the world; they are ever broadening their consciousness, ever seeking a higher and higher unity, ever approaching nearer to the one central Truth which is all-comprehensive.

Man's poverty is abysmal, his wants are endless till he becomes truly conscious of his soul. Till then, the world to him is in a state of continual flux– a phantasm that is and is not. For a man who has realised his soul there is a determinate centre of the universe around which all else can find its proper place, and from thence only can he draw and enjoy the blessedness of a harmonious life.

There was a time when the earth was only a nebulous mass whose particles were scattered far apart through the expanding force of heat; when she had not yet attained her definiteness of form and had neither beauty nor purpose, but only heat and motion. Gradually, when her vapours were condensed into a unified rounded whole through a force that strove to bring all straggling matters under the control of a centre, she occupied her proper place among the planets of the solar system, like an emerald pendant in a necklace of diamonds. So with our soul. When the heat and motion of blind impulses and passions distract it on all sides, we can neither give nor receive anything truly. But when we find our centre in our soul by the power of self-restraint, by the force that harmonises all warring elements and unifies those that are apart, then all our isolated impressions reduce themselves to wisdom, and all our momentary impulses of heart find their completion in love; then all the petty details of our life reveal an infinite purpose, and all our thoughts and deeds unite themselves inseparably in an internal harmony.

The Upanishads say with great emphasis, *Know thou the One, the Soul.*[21] *It is the bridge leading to the immortal being.*[22]

21. Tamēvaikam jānatha ātmānam.

22. Amritasyaisha sētuh.

This is the ultimate end of man, to find the *One* which is in him; which is his truth, which is his soul; the key with which he opens the gate of the spiritual life, the heavenly kingdom. His desires are many, and madly they run after the varied objects of the world, for therein they have their life and fulfilment. But that which is *one* in him is ever seeking for unity–unity in knowledge, unity in love, unity in purposes of will; its highest joy is when it reaches the infinite one within its eternal unity. Hence the saying of the Upanishad, *Only those of tranquil minds, and none else, can attain abiding joy, by realising within their souls the Being who manifests one essence in a multiplicity of forms.*[23]

Through all the diversities of the world the one in us is threading its course towards the one in all; this is its nature and this is its joy. But by that devious path it could never reach its goal if it had not a light of its own by which it could catch the sight of what it was seeking in a flash. The vision of the Supreme One in our own soul is a direct and immediate intuition, not based on any ratiocination or demonstration at all. Our eyes naturally see an object as a whole, not by breaking it up into parts, but by bringing all the parts together into a unity with ourselves. So with the intuition of our Soul-consciousness, which naturally and totally realises its unity in the Supreme One.

Says the Upanishad: *This deity who is manifesting himself in the activities of the universe always dwells in the heart of man as the supreme soul. Those who realise him through the immediate perception of the heart attain immortality.*[24]

---

23. Ēkam rūpam bahudhā yah karōtitam ātmastham yē anupaçyanti dīhrāh, tēshām sukham çāçvatam nētarēshām.

24. Ēsha dēvō vishvakarmā mahātmā sadā janānām hridayē sannivishtah. Hridā manīsha manasābhiklriptō ya ētad viduramritāstē bhavanti.

He is *Vishvakarma*; that is, in a multiplicity of forms and forces lies his outward manifestation in nature; but his inner manifestation in our soul is that which exists in unity. Our pursuit of truth in the domain of nature therefore is through analysis and the gradual methods of science, but our apprehension of truth in our soul is immediate and through direct intuition. We cannot attain the supreme soul by successive additions of knowledge acquired bit by bit even through all eternity, because he is one, he is not made up of parts; we can only know him as heart of our hearts and soul of our soul; we can only know him in the love and joy we feel when we give up our self and stand before him face to face.

The deepest and the most earnest prayer that has ever risen from the human heart has been uttered in our ancient tongue: O *thou self-revealing one, reveal thyself in me.*[25] We are in misery because we are creatures of self–the self that is unyielding and narrow, that reflects no light, that is blind to the infinite. Our self is loud with its own discordant clamour–it is not the tuned harp whose chords vibrate with the music of the eternal. Sighs of discontent and weariness of failure, idle regrets for the past and anxieties for the future are troubling our shallow hearts because we have not found our souls, and the self-revealing spirit has not been manifest within us. Hence our cry, O *thou awful one, save me with thy smile of grace ever and evermore.*[26] It is a stifling shroud of death, this self-gratification, this insatiable greed, this pride of possession, this insolent alienation of heart. *Rudra,* O *thou awful one, rend this dark cover in twain and let the saving beam of thy smile of grace strike through this night of gloom and waken my soul.*

From unreality lead me to the real, from darkness to the light, from death to immortality.[27] But how can one hope to

25. Āvirāvīrmayēdhi.
26. Rudra yat tē dakshinam mukham tēna mām pāhi nityam.
27. Asatōmā sadgamaya, tamasōmā jyōtirgamaya, mrityōrma mritangamaya.

have this prayer granted? For infinite is the distance that lies between truth and untruth, between death and deathlessness. Yet this measureless gulf is bridged in a moment when the self revealing one reveals himself in the soul. There the miracle happens, for there is the meeting-ground of the finite and infinite. *Father, completely sweep away all my sins!*[28] For in sin man takes part with the finite against the infinite that is in him. It is the defeat of his soul by his self. It is a perilously losing game, in which man stakes his all to gain a part. Sin is the blurring of truth which clouds the purity of our consciousness. In sin we lust after pleasures, not because they are truly desirable, but because the red light of our passions makes them appear desirable; we long for things not because they are great in themselves, but because our greed exaggerates them and makes them appear great. These exaggerations, these falsifications of the perspective of things, break the harmony of our life at every step; we lose the true standard of values and are distracted by the false claims of the varied interests of life contending with one another. It is this failure to bring all the elements of his nature under the unity and control of the Supreme One that makes man feel the pang of his separation from God and gives rise to the earnest prayer, O God, O Father, *completely sweep away all our sins.*[29] *Give unto us that which is good*[30] , the good which is the daily bread of our souls. In our pleasures we are confined to ourselves, in the good we are freed and we belong to all. As the child in its mother's womb gets its sustenance through the union of its life with the larger life of its mother, so our soul is nourished only through the good which is the recognition of its inner kinship, the channel of its communication with the infinite by which it is surrounded and fed. Hence it is said, "Blessed are they which do hunger and thirst after righteousness: for they shall be filled." For righ-

28. Vishvānidēva savitar duratāni parāsuva.

29. Vishvāni dēva savitar duritāni parāsuva.

30. Yad bhadram tanna āsuva.

teousness is the divine food of the soul; nothing but this can fill him, can make him live the life of the infinite, can help him in his growth towards the eternal. *We bow to thee from whom come the enjoyments of our life.*[31] *We bow also to thee from whom comes the good of our soul.*[32] We bow to thee who art good, the highest good[33] in whom we are united with everything, that is, in peace and harmony, in goodness and love.

Man's cry is to reach his fullest expression. It is this desire for self-expression that leads him to seek wealth and power. But he has to discover that accumulation is not realisation. It is the inner light that reveals him, not outer things. When this light is lighted, then in a moment he knows that Man's highest revelation is God's own revelation in him. And his cry is for this–the manifestation of his soul, which is the manifestation of God in his soul. Man becomes perfect man, he attains his fullest expression, when his soul realises itself in the Infinite being who is *Āvih* whose very essence is expression.

The real misery of man is in the fact that he has not fully come out, that he is self-obscured, lost in the midst of his own desires. He cannot feel himself beyond his personal surroundings, his greater self is blotted out, his truth is unrealised. The prayer that rises up from his whole being is therefore, *Thou, who art the spirit of manifestation, manifest thyself in me.*[34] This longing for the perfect expression of his self is more deeply inherent in man than his hunger and thirst for bodily sustenance, his lust for wealth and distinction. This prayer is not merely one born individually of him; it is in depth of all things, it is the ceaseless urging in him of the *Āvih*, of the spirit of eternal manifestation. The revealment of the infinite in the finite, which is the motive of all creation, is not seen in

---

31. Namah sambhavāya.
32. Namah çankarāyacha.
33. Namah çivāyacha, çivatarāya cha.
34. Āvirāvīrmayēdhi.

its perfection in the starry heavens, in the beauty of flowers. It is in the soul of man. For there will seeks its manifestation in will, and freedom turns to win its final prize in the freedom of surrender.

Therefore, it is the self of man which the great King of the universe has not shadowed with his throne—he has left it free. In his physical and mental organism, where man is related with nature, he has to acknowledge the rule of his King, but in his self he is free to disown him. There our God must win his entrance. There he comes as a guest, not as a king, and therefore he has to wait till he is invited. It is the man's self from which God has withdrawn his commands, for there he comes to court our love. His armed force, the laws of nature, stand outside its gate, and only beauty, the messenger of his love, finds admission within its precincts.

It is only in this region of will that anarchy is permitted; only in man's self that the discord of untruth and unrighteousness hold its reign; and things can come to such a pass that we may cry out in our anguish, "Such utter lawlessness could never prevail if there were a God!" Indeed, God has stood aside from our self, where his watchful patience knows no bounds, and where he never forces open the doors if shut against him. For this self of ours has to attain its ultimate meaning, which is the soul, not through the compulsion of God's power but through love, and thus become united with God in freedom.

He whose spirit has been made one with God stands before man as the supreme flower of humanity. There man finds in truth what he is; for there the *Āvih* is revealed to him in the soul of man as the most perfect revelation for him of God; for there we see the union of the supreme will with our will, our love with the love everlasting.

Therefore, in our country he who truly loves God receives such homage from men as would be considered almost sacrilegious in the west. We see in him God's wish fulfilled, the most difficult of all obstacles to his revealment removed, and God's own perfect joy fully blossoming in humanity. Through him we find the whole world of man overspread with a divine homeliness. His life, burning with God's love, makes all our earthly love resplendent. All the intimate associations of our life, all its experience of pleasure and pain, group themselves around this display of the divine love, and from the drama that we witness in him. The touch of an infinite mystery passes over the trivial and the familiar, making it break out into ineffable music. The trees and the stars and the blue hills appear to us as symbols aching with a meaning which can never be uttered in words. We seem to watch the Master in the very act of creation of a new world when a man's soul draws her heavy curtain of self aside, when her veil is lifted and she is face to face with her eternal lover.

But what is this state? It is like a morning of spring, varied in its life and beauty, yet one and entire. When a man's life rescued from distractions finds its unity in the soul, then the consciousness of the infinite becomes at once direct and natural to it as the light is to the flame. All the conflicts and contradictions of life are reconciled; knowledge, love and action harmonized; pleasure and pain become one in beauty, enjoyment and renunciation equal in goodness; the breach between the finite and the infinite fills with love and overflows; every moment carries its message of the eternal; the formless appears to us in the form of the flower, of the fruit; the boundless takes us up in his arms as a father and walks by our side as a friend. It is only the soul, the One in man which by its very nature can overcome all limits, and finds its affinity with the Supreme One. While yet we have not attained the internal harmony, and the wholeness of our being, our life remains a life of habits. The world still appears to us as a machine, to be mastered where it is useful, to be guarded against where it is dangerous, and never to be known in its full fellowship with us, alike in its physical nature and in its spiritual life and beauty.

III

THE PROBLEM OF EVIL

The question why there is evil in existence is the same as why there is imperfection, or, in other words, why there is creation at all. We must take it for granted that it could not be otherwise; that creation must be imperfect, must be gradual, and that it is futile to ask the question, Why we are?

But this is the real question we ought to ask: Is this imperfection the final truth, is evil absolute and ultimate? The river has its boundaries, its banks, but is a river all banks? or are the banks the final facts about the river? Do not these obstructions themselves give its water an onward motion? The towing rope binds a boat, but is the bondage its meaning? Does it not at the same time draw the boat forward?

The current of the world has its boundaries, otherwise it could have no existence, but its purpose is not shown in the boundaries which restrain it, but in its movement, which is towards perfection. The wonder is not that there should be obstacles and sufferings in this world, but that there should be law and order, beauty and joy, goodness and love. The idea of God that man has in his being is the wonder of all wonders. He has felt in the depths of his life that what appears as imperfect is the manifestation of the perfect; just as a man who has an ear for music realises the perfection of a song, while in fact he is only listening to a succession of notes. Man has found out the great paradox that what is limited is not imprisoned within its limits; it is ever moving, and therewith shedding its finitude every moment. In fact, imperfection is not a negation of perfectness; finitude is not contradictory to infinity: they are but completeness manifested in parts, infinity revealed within bounds.

Pain, which is the feeling of our finiteness, is not a fixture in our life. It is not an end in itself, as joy is. To meet with it is to know that it has no part in the true permanence of creation. It is what error is in our intellectual life. To go through the history of the development of science is to go through the maze of mistakes it made current at different times. Yet no one really believes that science is the one perfect mode of disseminating mistakes. The progressive ascertainment of truth is the important thing to remember in the history of science, not its innumerable mistakes. Error, by its nature, cannot be stationary; it cannot remain with truth; like a tramp, it must quit its lodging as soon as it fails to pay its score to the full.

As in intellectual error, so in evil of any other form, its essence is impermanence, for it cannot accord with the whole. Every moment it is being corrected by the totality of things and keeps changing its aspect. We exaggerate its importance by imagining it as a standstill. Could we collect the statistics of the immense amount of death and putrefaction happening every moment in this earth, they would appal us. But evil is ever moving; with all its incalculable immensity it does not effectually clog the current of our life; and we find that the earth, water, and air remain sweet and pure for living beings. All statistics consist of our attempts to represent statistically what is in motion; and in the process things assume a weight in our mind which they have not in reality. For this reason a man, who by his profession is concerned with any particular aspect of life, is apt to magnify its proportions; in laying undue stress upon facts he loses his hold upon truth. A detective may have the opportunity of studying crimes in detail, but he loses his sense of their relative places in the whole social economy. When science collects facts to illustrate the struggle for existence that is going on in the kingdom of life, it raises a picture in our minds of "nature red in tooth and claw." But in these mental pictures we give a fixity to colours and forms which are really evanescent. It is like calculating the weight of the air on each square inch of our body to prove that it must be crushingly heavy for us. With every weight, however, there is an adjustment, and we lightly bear our burden. With the struggle for existence in nature there is reciprocity. There is the love for children and for comrades; there is the sacrifice of self, which springs from love; and this love is the positive element in life.

If we kept the search-light of our observation turned upon the fact of death, the world would appear to us like a huge charnel-house; but in the world of life the thought of death has, we find, the least possible hold upon our minds. Not because it is the least apparent, but because it is the negative aspect of life; just as, in spite of the fact that we shut our eyelids every second, it is the openings of the eye that count. Life as a whole never takes death seriously. It laughs, dances and plays, it builds, hoards and loves in death's face. Only when we detach one individual fact of death do we see its blankness and become dismayed. We lose sight of the wholeness of a life of which death is part. It is like looking at a piece of cloth through a microscope. It appears like a net; we gaze at the big holes and shiver in imagination. But the truth is, death is not the ultimate reality. It looks black, as the sky looks blue; but it does not blacken existence, just as the sky does not leave its stain upon the wings of the bird.

When we watch a child trying to walk, we see its countless failures; its successes are but few. If we had to limit our observation within a narrow space of time, the sight would be cruel. But we find that in spite of its repeated failures there is an impetus of joy in the child which sustains it in its seemingly impossible task. We see it does not think of its falls so much as of its power to keep its balance though for only a moment.

Like these accidents in a child's attempts to walk, we meet with sufferings in various forms in our life every day, showing the imperfections in our knowledge and our available power, and in the application of our will. But if these revealed our weakness to us only, we should die of utter depression. When we select for observation a limited area of our activities, our individual failures and miseries loom large in our minds; but our life leads us instinctively to take a wider view. It gives us an ideal of perfection which ever carries us beyond our present limitations. Within us we have a hope which always walks in front of our present narrow experience; it is the undying faith in the infinite in us; it will never accept any of our disabilities as a permanent fact; it sets no limit to its own scope; it dares to assert that man has oneness with God; and its wild dreams become true every day.

We see the truth when we set our mind towards the infinite. The ideal of truth is not in the narrow present, not in our immediate sensations, but in the consciousness of the whole which give us a taste of what we *should* have in what we *do* have. Consciously or unconsciously we have in our life this feeling of Truth which is ever larger than its appearance; for our life is facing the infinite, and it is in movement. Its aspiration is therefore infinitely more than its achievement, and as it goes on it finds that no realisation of truth ever leaves it stranded on the desert of finality, but carries it to a region beyond. Evil cannot altogether arrest the course of life on the highway and rob it of its possessions. For the evil has to pass on, it has to grow into good; it cannot stand and give battle to the All. If the least evil could stop anywhere indefinitely, it would sink deep and cut into the very roots of existence. As it is, man does not really believe in evil, just as he cannot believe that violin strings have been purposely made to create the exquisite torture of discordant notes, though by the aid of statistics it can be mathematically proved that the probability of discord is far greater than that of harmony, and for one who can play the violin there are thousands who cannot. The potentiality of perfection outweighs actual contradictions. No doubt there have been people who asserted existence to be an absolute evil, but man can never take them seriously. Their pessimism is a mere pose, either intellectual or sentimental; but life itself is optimistic: it wants to go on. Pessimism is a form of mental dipsomania, it disdains healthy nourishment, indulges in the strong drink of denunciation, and creates an artificial dejection which thirsts for a stronger draught. If existence were an evil, it would wait for no philosopher to prove it. It is like convicting a man of suicide, while all the time he stands before you in the flesh. Existence itself is here to prove that it cannot be an evil.

An imperfection which is not all imperfection, but which has perfection for its ideal, must go through a perpetual realisation. Thus, it is the function of our intellect to realise the truth through untruths, and knowledge is nothing but the continually burning up of error to set free the light of truth. Our will, our character, has to attain perfection by continually overcoming evils, either inside or outside us, or both; our physical life is consuming bodily materials every moment to maintain the life fire; and our moral life too has its fuel to burn. This life process is going on—we know it, we have felt it; and we have a faith which no individual instances to the contrary can shake, that the direction of humanity is from evil to good. For we feel that good is the positive element in man's nature, and in every age and every clime what man values most is his ideals of goodness. We have known the good, we have loved it, and we have paid our highest reverence to men who have shown in their lives what goodness is.

The question will be asked, What is goodness; what does our moral nature mean? My answer is, that when a man begins to have an extended vision of his self, when he realises that he is much more than at present he seems to be, he begins to get conscious of his moral nature. Then he grows aware of that which he is yet to be, and the state not yet experienced by him becomes more real than that under his direct experience. Necessarily, his perspective of life changes, and his will takes the place of his wishes. For will is the supreme wish of the larger life, the life whose greater portion is out of our present reach, most of whose objects are not before our sight. Then comes the conflict of our lesser man with our greater man, of our wishes with our will, of the desire for things affecting our senses with the purpose that is within our heart. Then we begin to distinguish between what we immediately desire and what is good. For good is that which is desirable for our greater self. Thus the sense of goodness comes out of a truer view of our life, which is the connected view of the wholeness of the field of life, and which takes into account not only what is present before us but what is not, and perhaps never humanly can be. Man, who is provident, feels for that life of his which is not yet existent, feels much more that than for the life that is with him; therefore he is ready to sacrifice his present inclination for the unrealised future. In this he becomes great, for he realises truth. Even to be efficiently selfish one has to recognise this truth, and has to curb his immediate impulses—in other words, has to be moral. For our moral faculty is the faculty by which we know that life is not made up of fragments, purposeless and discontinuous. This moral sense of man not only gives him the power to see that the self has a continuity in time, but it also enables him to see that he is not true when he is only restricted to his own self. He is more in truth than he is in fact. He truly belongs to individuals who are not included in his own individuality, and whom he is never even likely to know. As he has a feeling for his future self which is outside his present consciousness, so he has a feeling for his greater self which is outside the limits of his personality. There is no man who has not this feeling to some extent, who has never sacrificed his selfish desire for the sake of some other person, who has never felt a pleasure in undergoing some loss or trouble because it pleased somebody else. It is a truth that man is not a detached being, that he has a universal aspect; and when he recognises this he becomes great. Even the most evilly-disposed selfishness has to recognise this when it seeks the power to do evil; for it cannot ignore truth and yet be strong. So in order to claim the aid of truth, selfishness has to be unselfish to some extent. A band of robbers must be moral in order to hold together as a band; they may rob the whole world but not each other. To make an immoral intention successful, some of its weapons must be moral. In fact, very often it is our very moral strength which gives us most effectively the power to do evil, to exploit other individuals for our own benefit, to rob other people of their rights. The life of an animal is unmoral, for it is aware only of an immediate present; the life of a man can be immoral, but that only means that it must have a moral basis. What is immoral is imperfectly moral, just as what is false is true to a small extent, or it cannot even be false. Not to see is to be blind, but to see wrongly is to see only in an imperfect manner. Man's selfishness is a beginning to see some connection, some purpose in life; and to act in accordance with its dictates requires self-restraint and regulation of conduct. A selfish man willingly undergoes troubles for the sake of the self, he suffers hardship and privation without a murmur, simply because he knows that what is pain and trouble, looked at from the point of view of a short space of time, are just the opposite when seen in a larger perspective. Thus what is a loss to the smaller man is a gain to the greater, and *vice versa*.

To the man who lives for an idea, for his country, for the good of humanity, life has an extensive meaning, and to that extent pain becomes less important to him. To live the life of goodness is to live the life of all. Pleasure is for one's own self, but goodness is concerned with the happiness of all humanity and for all time. From the point of view of the good, pleasure and pain appear in a different meaning; so much so, that pleasure may be shunned, and pain be courted in its place, and death itself be made welcome as giving a higher value to life. From these higher standpoints of a man's life, the standpoints of the good, pleasure and pain lose their absolute value. Martyrs prove it in history, and we prove it every day in our life in our little martyrdoms. When we take a pitcherful of water from the sea it has its weight, but when we take a dip into the sea itself a thousand pitchersful of water flow above our head, and we do not feel their weight. We have to carry the pitcher of self with our strength; and so, while on the plane of selfishness pleasure and pain have their full weight, on the moral plane they are so much lightened that the man who has reached it appears to us almost superhuman in his patience under crushing trails, and his forbearance in the face of malignant persecution.

To live in perfect goodness is to realise one's life in the infinitive. This is the most comprehensive view of life which we can have by our inherent power of the moral vision of the wholeness of life. And the teaching of Buddha is to cultivate this moral power to the highest extent, to know that our field of activities is not bound to the plane of our narrow self. This is the vision of the heavenly kingdom of Christ. When we attain to that universal life, which is the moral life, we become freed from the bonds of pleasure and pain, and the place vacated by our self becomes filled with an unspeakable joy which springs from measureless love. In this state the soul's activity is all the more heightened, only its motive power is not from desires, but in its own joy. This is the *Karma-yoga* of the *Gita*, the way to become one with the infinite activity by the exercise of the activity of disinterested goodness.

When Buddha mentioned upon the way of realising mankind from the grip of misery he came to this truth: that when man attains his highest end by merging the individual in the universal, he becomes free from the thraldom of pain. Let us consider this point more fully.

A student of mine once related to me his adventure in a storm, and complained that all the time he was troubled with the feeling that this great commotion in nature behaved to him as if he were no more than a mere handful of dust. That he was a distinct personality with a will of his own had not the least influence upon what was happening.

I said, "If consideration for our individuality could sway nature from her path, then it would be the individuals who would suffer most."

But he persisted in his doubt, saying that there was this fact which could not be ignored–the feeling that I am. The "I" in us seeks for a relation which is individual to it.

I replied that the relation of the "I" is with something which is "not-I." So we must have a medium which is common to both, and we must be absolutely certain that it is the same to the "I" as it is to the "not-I."

This is what needs repeating here. We have to keep in mind that our individuality by its nature is impelled to seek for the universal. Our body can only die if it tries to eat its own substance, and our eye loses the meaning of its function if it can only see itself.

Just as we find that the stronger the imagination the less is it merely imaginary and the more is it in harmony with truth, so we see the more vigorous our individuality the more does it widen towards the universal. For the greatness of a personality is not in itself but in its content, which is universal, just as the depth of a lake is judged not by the size of its cavity but by the depth of its water.

So, if it is a truth that the yearning of our nature is for reality, and that our personality cannot be happy with a fantastic universe of its own creation, then it is clearly best for it that our will can only deal with things by following their law, and cannot do with them just as it pleases. This unyielding sureness of reality sometimes crosses our will, and very often leads us to disaster, just as the firmness of the earth invariably hurts the falling child who is learning to walk. Nevertheless it is the same firmness that hurts him which makes his walking possible. Once, while passing under a bridge, the mast of my boat got stuck in one of its girders. If only for a moment the mast would have bent an inch or two, or the bridge raised its back like a yawning cat, or the river given in, it would have been all right with me. But they took no notice of my helplessness. That is the very reason why I could make use of the river, and sail upon it with the help of the mast, and that is why, when its current was inconvenient, I could rely upon the bridge. Things are what they are, and we have to know them if we would deal with them, and knowledge of them is possible because our wish is not their law. This knowledge is a joy to us, for the knowledge is one of the channels of our relation with the things outside us; it is making them our own, and thus widening the limit of our self.

At every step we have to take into account others than ourselves. For only in death are we alone. A poet is a true poet when he can make his personal idea joyful to all men, which he could not do if he had not a medium common to all his audience. This common language has its own law which the poet must discover and follow, by doing which he becomes true and attains poetical immortality.

We see then that man's individuality is not his highest truth; there is that in him which is universal. If he were made to live in a world where his own self was the only factor to consider, then that would be the worst prison imaginable to him, for man's deepest joy is in growing greater and greater by more and more union with the all. This, as we have seen, would be an impossibility if there were no law common to all. Only by discovering the law and following it, do we become great, do we realise the universal; while, so long as our individual desires are at conflict with the universal law, we suffer pain and are futile.

There was a time when we prayed for special concessions, we expected that the laws of nature should be held in abeyance for our own convenience. But now we know better. We know that law cannot be set aside, and in this knowledge we have become strong. For this law is not something apart from us; it is our own. The universal power which is manifested in the universal law is one with our own power. It will thwart us where we are small, where we are against the current of things; but it will help us where we are great, where we are in unison with the all. Thus, through the help of science, as we come to know more of the laws of nature, we gain in power; we tend to attain a universal body. Our organ of sight, our organ of locomotion, our physical strength becomes world-wide; steam and electricity become our nerve and muscle. Thus we find that, just as throughout our bodily organisation there is a principle of relation by virtue of which we can call the entire body our own, and can use it as such, so all through the universe there is that principle of uninterrupted relation by virtue of which we can call the whole world our extended body and use it accordingly. And in this age of science it is our endeavour fully to establish our claim to our world-self. We know all our poverty and sufferings are owing to our inability to realise this legitimate claim of ours. Really, there is no limit to our powers, for we are not outside the universal power which is the expression of universal law. We are on our way to overcome disease and death, to conquer pain and poverty; for through scientific knowledge we are ever on our way to realise the universal in its physical aspect. And as we make progress we find that pain, disease, and poverty of power are not absolute, but that is only the want of adjustment of our individual self to our universal self which gives rise to them.

It is the same with our spiritual life. When the individual man in us chafes against the lawful rule of the universal man we become morally small, and we must suffer. In such a condition our successes are our greatest failures, and the very fulfilment of our desires leaves us poorer. We hanker after special gains for ourselves, we want to enjoy privileges which none else can share with us. But everything that is absolutely special must keep up a perpetual warfare with what is general. In such a state of civil war man always lives behind barricades, and in any civilisation which is selfish our homes are not real homes, but artificial barriers around us. Yet we complain that we are not happy, as if there were something inherent in the nature of things to make us miserable. The universal spirit is waiting to crown us with happiness, but our individual spirit would not accept it. It is our life of the self that causes conflicts and complications everywhere, upsets the normal balance of society and gives rise to miseries of all kinds. It brings things to such a pass that to maintain order we have to create artificial coercions and organised forms of tyranny, and tolerate infernal institutions in our midst, whereby at every moment humanity is humiliated.

We have seen that in order to be powerful we have to submit to the laws of the universal forces, and to realise in practice that they are our own. So, in order to be happy, we have to submit our individual will to the sovereignty of the universal will, and to feel in truth that it is our own will. When we reach that state wherein the adjustment of the finite in us to the infinite is made perfect, then pain itself becomes a valuable asset. It becomes a measuring rod with which to gauge the true value of our joy.

The most important lesson that man can learn from his life is not that there *is* pain in this world, but that it depends upon him to turn it into good account, that it is possible for him to transmute it into joy. The lesson has not been lost altogether to us, and there is no man living who would willingly be deprived of his right to suffer pain, for that is his right to be a man. One day the wife of a poor labourer complained bitterly to me that her eldest boy was going to be sent away to a rich relative's house for part of the year. It was the implied kind intention of trying to relieve her of her trouble that gave her the shock, for a mother's trouble is a mother's own by her inalienable right of love, and she was not going to surrender it to any dictates of expediency. Man's freedom is never in being saved troubles, but it is the freedom to take trouble for his own good, to make the trouble an element in his joy. It can be made so only when we realise that our individual self is not the highest meaning of our being, that in us we have the world-man who is immortal, who is not afraid of death or sufferings, and who looks upon pain as only the other side of joy. He who has realised this knows that it is pain which is our true wealth as imperfect beings, and has made us great and worthy to take our seat with the perfect. He knows that we are not beggars; that it is the hard coin which must be paid for everything valuable in this life, for our power, our wisdom, our love; that in pain is symbolised the infinite possibility of perfection, the eternal unfolding of joy; and the man who loses all pleasure in accepting pain sinks down and down to the lowest depth of penury and degradation. It is only when we invoke the aid of pain for our self-gratification that she becomes evil and takes her vengeance for the insult done to her by hurling us into misery. For she is the vestal virgin consecrated to the service of the immortal perfection, and when she takes her true place before the altar of the infinite she casts off her dark veil and bares her face to the beholder as a revelation of supreme joy.

IV

THE PROBLEM OF SELF

At one pole of my being I am one with stocks and stones. There I have to acknowledge the rule of universal law. That is where the foundation of my existence lies, deep down below. Its strength lies in its being held firm in the clasp of comprehensive world, and in the fullness of its community with all things.

But at the other pole of my being I am separate from all. There I have broken through the cordon of equality and stand alone as an individual. I am absolutely unique, I am I, I am incomparable. The whole weight of the universe cannot crush out this individuality of mine. I maintain it in spite of the tremendous gravitation of all things. It is small in appearance but great in reality. For it holds its own against the forces that would rob it of its distinction and make it one with the dust.

This is the superstructure of the self which rises from the indeterminate depth and darkness of its foundation into the open, proud of its isolation, proud of having given shape to a single individual idea of the architect's which has no duplicate in the whole universe. If this individuality be demolished, then though no material be lost, not an atom destroyed, the creative joy which was crystallised therein is gone. We are absolutely bankrupt if we are deprived of this specialty, this individuality, which is the only thing we can call our own; and which, if lost, is also a loss to the whole world. It is most valuable because it is not universal. And therefore only through it can we gain the universe more truly than if we were lying within its breast unconscious of our distinctiveness. The universal is ever seeking its consummation in the unique. And the desire we have to keep our uniqueness intact is really the desire of the universe acting in us. It is our joy of the infinite in us that gives us our joy in ourselves.

That this separateness of self is considered by man as his most precious possession is proved by the sufferings he undergoes and the sins he commits for its sake. But the consciousness of separation has come from the eating of the fruit of knowledge. It has led man to shame and crime and death; yet it is dearer to him than any paradise where the self lies, securely slumbering in perfect innocence in the womb of mother nature.

It is a constant striving and suffering for us to maintain the separateness of this self of ours. And in fact it is this suffering which measures its value. One side of the value is sacrifice, which represents how much the cost has been. The other side of it is the attainment, which represents how much has been gained. If the self meant nothing to us but pain and sacrifice, it could have no value for us, and on no account would we willingly undergo such sacrifice. In such case there could be no doubt at all that the highest object of humanity would be the annihilation of self.

But if there is a corresponding gain, if it does not end in a void but in a fullness, then it is clear that its negative qualities, its very sufferings and sacrifices, make it all the more precious. That it is so has been proved by those who have realised the positive significance of self, and have accepted its responsibilities with eagerness and undergone sacrifices without flinching.

With the foregoing introduction it will be easy for me to answer the question once asked by one of my audience as to whether the annihilation of self has not been held by India as the supreme goal of humanity?

In the first place we must keep in mind the fact that man is never literal in the expression of his ideas, except in matters most trivial. Very often man's words are not a language at all, but merely a vocal gesture of the dumb. They may indicate, but do not express his thoughts. The more vital his thoughts the more have his words to be explained by the context of his life. Those who seek to know his meaning by the aid of the dictionary only technically reach the house, for they are stopped by the outside wall and find no entrance to the hall. This is the reason why the teachings of our greatest prophets give rise to endless disputations when we try to understand them by following their words and not be realising them in our own lives. The men who are cursed with the gift of the literal mind are the unfortunate ones who are always busy with their nets and neglect the fishing.

It is not only in Buddhism and the Indian religions, but in Christianity too, that the ideal of selflessness is preached with all fervour. In the last the symbol of death has been used for expressing the idea of man's deliverance from the life which is not true. This is the same as Nirvnāna, the symbol of the extinction of the lamp.

In the typical thought of India it is held that the true deliverance of man is the deliverance from *avidyā*, from ignorance. It is not in destroying anything that is positive and real, for that cannot be possible, but that which is negative, which obstructs our vision of truth. When this obstruction, which is ignorance, is removed, then only is the eyelid drawn up which is no loss to the eye.

It is our ignorance which makes us think that our self, as self, is real, that it has its complete meaning in itself. When we take that wrong view of self then we try to live in such a manner as to make self the ultimate object of our life. Then we are doomed to disappointment like the man who tries to reach his destination by firmly clutching the dust of the road. Our self has no means of holding us, for its own nature is to pass on; and by clinging to this thread of self which is passing through the loom of life we cannot make it serve the purpose of the cloth into which it is being woven. When a man, with elaborate care, arranges for an enjoyment of the self, he lights a fire but has no dough to make his bread with; the fire flares up and consumes itself to extinction, like an unnatural beast that eats its own progeny and dies.

In an unknown language the words are tyrannically prominent. They stop us but say nothing. To be rescued from this fetter of words we must rid ourselves of the *avidyā*, our ignorance, and then our mind will find its freedom in the inner idea. But it would be foolish to say that our ignorance of the language can be dispelled only by the destruction of the words. No, when the perfect knowledge comes, every word remains in its place, only they do not bind us to themselves, but let us pass through them and lead us to the idea which is emancipation.

Thus it is only *avidyā* which makes the self our fetter by making us think that it is an end in itself, and by preventing our seeing that it contains the idea that transcends its limits. That is why the wise man comes and says, "Set yourselves free from the *avidyā*; know your true soul and be saved from the grasp of the self which imprisons you."

We gain our freedom when we attain our truest nature. The man who is an artist finds his artistic freedom when he finds his ideal of art. Then is he freed from laborious attempts at imitation, from the goadings of popular approbation. It is the function of religion not to destroy our nature but to fulfil it.

The Sanskrit word *dharma* which is usually translated into English as religion has a deeper meaning in our language. *Dharma* is the innermost nature, the essence, the implicit truth, of all things. *Dharma* is the ultimate purpose that is working in our self. When any wrong is done we say that *dharma* is violated, meaning that the lie has been given to our true nature.

But this *dharma*, which is the truth in us, is not apparent, because it is inherent. So much so, that it has been held that sinfulness is the nature of man, and only by the special grace of God can a particular person be saved. This is like saying that the nature of the seed is to remain enfolded within its shell, and it is only by some special miracle that it can be grown into a tree. But do we not know that the *appearance* of the seed contradicts its true nature? When you submit it to chemical analysis you may find in it carbon and proteid and a good many other things, but not the idea of a branching tree. Only when the tree begins to take shape do you come to see its *dharma*, and then you can affirm without doubt that the seed which has been wasted and allowed to rot in the ground has been thwarted in its *dharma*, in the fulfilment of its true nature. In the history of humanity we have known the living seed in us to sprout. We have seen the great purpose in us taking shape in the lives of our greatest men, and have felt certain that though there are numerous individual lives that seem ineffectual, still it is not their *dharma* to remain barren; but it is for them to burst their cover and transform themselves into a vigorous spiritual shoot, growing up into the air and light, and branching out in all directions.

The freedom of the seed is in the attainment of its *dharma*, its nature and destiny of becoming a tree; it is the non-accomplishment which is its prison. The sacrifice by which a thing attains its fulfilment is not a sacrifice which ends in death; it is the casting-off of bonds which wins freedom.

When we know the highest ideal of freedom which a man has, we know his *dharma*, the essence of his nature, the real meaning of his self. At first sight it seems that man counts that as freedom by which he gets unbounded opportunities of self gratification and self-aggrandisement. But surely this is not borne out by history. Our revelatory men have always been those who have lived the life of self-sacrifice. The higher nature in man always seeks for something which transcends itself and yet is its deepest truth; which claims all its sacrifice, yet makes this sacrifice its own recompense. This is man's *dharma*, man's religion, and man's self is the vessel which is to carry this sacrifice to the altar.

We can look at our self in its two different aspects. The self which displays itself, and the self which transcends itself and thereby reveals its own meaning. To display itself it tries to be big, to stand upon the pedestal of its accumulations, and to retain everything to itself. To reveal itself it gives up everything it has; thus becoming perfect like a flower that has blossomed out from the bud, pouring from its chalice of beauty all its sweetness.

The lamp contains its oil, which it holds securely in its close grasp and guards from the least loss. Thus is it separate from all other objects around it and is miserly. But when lighted it finds its meaning at once; its relation with all things far and near is established, and it freely sacrifices its fund of oil to feed the flame.

Such a lamp is our self. So long as it hoards its possessions it keeps itself dark, its conduct contradicts its true purpose. When it finds illumination it forgets itself in a moment, holds the light high, and serves it with everything it has; for therein is its revelation. This revelation is the freedom which Buddha preached. He asked the lamp to give up its oil. But purposeless giving up is a still darker poverty which he never could have meant. The lamp must give up its oil to the light and thus set free the purpose it has in its hoarding. This is emancipation. The path Buddha pointed out was not merely the practice of self-abnegation, but the widening of love. And therein lies the true meaning of Buddha's preaching.

When we find that the state of *Nirvāna* preached by Buddha is through love, then we know for certain that *Nirvāna* is the highest culmination of love. For love is an end unto itself. Everything else raises the question "Why?" in our mind, and we require a reason for it. But when we say, "I love," then there is no room for the "why"; it is the final answer in itself.

Doubtless, even selfishness impels one to give away. But the selfish man does it on compulsion. That is like plucking fruit when it is unripe; you have to tear it from the tree and bruise the branch. But when a man loves, giving becomes a matter of joy to him, like the tree's surrender of the ripe fruit. All our belongings assume a weight by the ceaseless gravitation of our selfish desires; we cannot easily cast them away from us. They seem to belong to our very nature, to stick to us as a second skin, and we bleed as we detach them. But when we are possessed by love, its force acts in the opposite direction. The things that closely adhered to us lose their adhesion and weight, and we find that they are not of us. Far from being a loss to give them away, we find in that the fulfilment of our being.

Thus we find in perfect love the freedom of our self. That only which is done for love is done freely, however much pain it may cause. Therefore working for love is freedom in action. This is the meaning of the teaching of disinterested work in the *Gīta*.

The *Gīta* says action we must have, for only in action do we manifest our nature. But this manifestation is not perfect so long as our action is not free. In fact, our nature is obscured by work done by the compulsion of want or fear. The mother reveals herself in the service of her children, so our true freedom is not the freedom *from* action but freedom *in* action, which can only be attained in the work of love.

God's manifestation is in his work of creation and it is said in the Upanishad, *Knowledge, power, and action are of his nature*[35] they are not imposed upon him from outside. Therefore his work is his freedom, and in his creation he realises himself. The same thing is said elsewhere in other words: *From joy does spring all this creation, by joy is it maintained, towards joy does it progress, and into joy does it enter.*[36] It means that God's creation has not its source in any necessity; it comes from his fullness of joy; it is his love that creates, therefore in creation is his own revealment.

The artist who has a joy in the fullness of his artistic idea objectifies it and thus gains it more fully by holding it afar. It is joy which detaches ourselves from us, and then gives it form in creations of love in order to make it more perfectly our own. Hence there must be this separation, not a separation of repulsion but a separation of love. Repulsion has only the one element, the element of severance. But love has two, the element of severance, which is only an appearance, and the element of union which is the ultimate truth. Just as when the father tosses his child up from his arms it has the appearance of rejection but its truth is quite the reverse.

So we must know that the meaning of our self is not to be found in its separateness from God and others, but in the ceaseless realisation of *yoga*, of union; not on the side of the

---

35. "Svābhāvikī jnāna bala kriyācha."
36. Ānandādhyēva khalvimāni bhūtāni jāyantē, ānandēna jātāni jīvanti, ānandamprayantyabhisamviçanti.

canvas where it is blank, but on the side where the picture is being painted.

This is the reason why the separateness of our self has been described by our philosophers as *māyā*, as an illusion, because it has no intrinsic reality of its own. It looks perilous; it raises its isolation to a giddy height and casts a black shadow upon the fair face of existence; from the outside it has an aspect of a sudden disruption, rebellious and destructive; it is proud, domineering and wayward; it is ready to rob the world of all its wealth to gratify its craving of a moment; to pluck with a reckless, cruel hand all the plumes from the divine bird of beauty to deck its ugliness for a day; indeed man's legend has it that it bears the black mark of disobedience stamped on its forehead for ever; but still all this *māyā*, envelopment of *avidyā*; it is the mist, it is not the sun; it is the black smoke that presages the fire of love.

Imagine some savage who, in his ignorance, thinks that it is the paper of the banknote that has the magic, by virtue of which the possessor of it gets all he wants. He piles up the papers, hides them, handles them in all sorts of absurd ways, and then at last, wearied by his efforts, comes to the sad conclusion that they are absolutely worthless, only fit to be thrown into the fire. But the wise man knows that the paper of the banknote is all *māyā*, and until it is given up to the bank it is futile. It is only *avidyā*, our ignorance, that makes us believe that the separateness of our self like the paper of the banknote is precious in itself, and by acting on this belief our self is rendered valueless. It is only when the *avidyā* is removed that this very self comes to us with a wealth which is priceless. For *He manifests Himself in forms which His joy assumes.*[37] These forms are separate from Him, and the value that these forms have is only what his joy has imparted to them. When we transfer back

37. Ānandarūpamamritam yadvibhāti.

these forms into that original joy, which is love, then we cash them in the bank and we find their truth.

When pure necessity drives man to his work it takes an accidental and contingent character, it becomes a mere makeshift arrangement; it is deserted and left in ruins when necessity changes its course. But when his work is the outcome of joy, the forms that it takes have the elements of immortality. The immortal in man imparts to it its own quality of permanence.

Our self, as a form of God's joy, is deathless. For his joy is *amritham*, eternal. This it is in us which makes us sceptical of death, even when the fact of death cannot be doubted. In reconcilement of this contradiction in us we come to the truth that in the dualism of death and life there is a harmony. We know that the life of a soul, which is finite in its expression and infinite in its principle, must go through the portals of death in its journey to realise the infinite. It is death which is monistic, it has no life in it. But life is dualistic; it has an appearance as well as truth; and death is that appearance, that *māyā*, which is an inseparable companion to life. Our self to live must go through a continual change and growth of form, which may be termed a continual death and a continual life going on at the same time. It is really courting death when we refuse to accept death; when we wish to give the form of the self some fixed changelessness; when the self feels no impulse which urges it to grow out of itself; when it treats its limits as final and acts accordingly. Then comes our teacher's call to die to this death; not a call to annihilation but to eternal life. It is the extinction of the lamp in the morning light; not the abolition of the sun. It is really asking us consciously to give effect to the innermost wish that we have in the depths of our nature.

We have a dual set of desires in our being, which it should be our endeavour to bring into a harmony. In the region of our physical nature we have one set of which we are conscious always. We wish to enjoy our food and drink, we hanker after bodily pleasure and comfort. These desires are self-centered; they are solely concerned with their respective impulses. The wishes of our palate often run counter to what our stomach can allow.

But we have another set, which is the desire of our physical system as a whole, of which we are usually unconscious. It is the wish for health. This is always doing its work, mending and repairing, making new adjustments in cases of accident, and skilfully restoring the balance wherever disturbed. It has no concern with the fulfilment of our immediate bodily desires, but it goes beyond the present time. It is the principle of our physical wholeness, it links our life with its past and its future and maintains the unity of its parts. He who is wise knows it, and makes his other physical wishes harmonise with it.

We have a greater body which is the social body. Society is an organism, of which we as parts have our individual wishes. We want our own pleasure and license. We want to pay less and gain more than anybody else. This causes scramblings and fights. But there is that other wish in us which does its work in the depths of the social being. It is the wish for the welfare of the society. It transcends the limits of the present and the personal. It is on the side of the infinite.

He who is wise tries to harmonise the wishes that seek for self-gratification with the wish for the social good, and only thus can he realise his higher self.

In its finite aspect the self is conscious of its separateness, and there it is ruthless in its attempt to have more distinction than all others. But in its infinite aspect its wish is to gain that harmony which leads to its perfection and not its mere aggrandisement.

The emancipation of our physical nature is in attaining health, of our social being in attaining goodness, and of our self in attaining love. This last is what Buddha describes as extinction–the extinction of selfishness–which is the function of love, and which does not lead to darkness but to illumination. This is the attainment of *bodhi*, or the true awakening; it is the revealing in us of the infinite joy by the light of love.

The passage of our self is through its selfhood, which is independent, to its attainment of soul, which is harmonious. This harmony can never be reached through compulsion. So our will, in the history of its growth, must come through independence and rebellion to the ultimate completion. We must have the possibility of the negative form of freedom, which is licence, before we can attain the positive freedom, which is love.

This negative freedom, the freedom of self-will, can turn its back upon its highest realisation, but it cannot cut itself away from it altogether, for then it will lose its own meaning. Our self-will has freedom up to a certain extent; it can know what it is to break away from the path, but it cannot continue in that direction indefinitely. For we are finite on our negative side. We must come to an end in our evil doing, in our career of discord. For evil is not infinite, and discord cannot be an end in itself. Our will has freedom in order that it may find out that its true course is towards goodness and love. For goodness and love are infinite, and only in the infinite is the perfect realisation of freedom possible. So our will can be free not towards the limitations of our self, not where it is *māyā* and negation, but towards the unlimited, where is truth and love. Our freedom cannot go against its own principle of freedom and yet be free; it cannot commit suicide and yet live. We cannot say that we should have infinite freedom to fetter ourselves, for the fettering ends the freedom.

So in the freedom of our will, we have the same dualism of appearance and truth—our self-will is only the appearance of freedom and love is the truth. When we try to make this appearance independent of truth, then our attempt brings misery and proves its own futility in the end. Everything has this dualism of *māyā* and *satyam*, appearance and truth. Words are *māyā* where they are merely sounds and finite, they are *satyam* where they are ideas and infinite. Our self is *māyā* where it is merely individual and finite, where it considers its separateness as absolute; it is *satyam* where it recognises its essence in the universal and infinite, in the supreme self, in *paramātman*. This is what Christ means when he says, "Before Abraham was I am." This is the eternal *I am* that speaks through the *I am* that is in me. The individual *I am* attains its perfect end when it realises its freedom of harmony in the infinite *I am*. Then is it *mukti*, its deliverance from the thraldom of *māyā*, of appearance, which springs from *avidyā*, from ignorance; its emancipation in *çāntam çivam advaitam*, in the perfect repose in truth, in the perfect activity in goodness, and in the perfect union in love.

Not only in our self but also in nature is there this separateness from God, which has been described as *māyā* by our philosophers, because the separateness does not exist by itself, it does not limit God's infinity from outside. It is his own will that has imposed limits to itself, just as the chess-player restricts his will with regard to the moving of the chessmen. The player willingly enters into definite relations with each particular piece and realises the joy of his power by these very restrictions. It is not that he cannot move the chessmen just as he pleases, but if he does so then there can be no play. If God assumes his rôle of omnipotence, then his creation is at an end and his power loses all its meaning. For power to be a power must act within limits. God's water must be water, his earth can never be other than earth. The law that has made them water and earth is his own law by which he has separated the play from the player, for therein the joy of the player consists.

As by the limits of law nature is separated from God, so it is the limits of its egoism which separates the self from him. He has willingly set limits to his will, and has given us mastery over the little world of our own. It is like a father's settling upon his son some allowance within the limit of which he is free to do what he likes. Though it remains a portion of the father's own property, yet he frees it from the operation of his own will. The reason of it is that the will, which is love's will and therefore free, can have its joy only in a union with another free will. The tyrant who must have slaves looks upon them as instruments of his purpose. It is the consciousness of his own necessity which makes him crush the will out of them, to make his self-interest absolutely secure. This self-interest cannot brook the least freedom in others, because it is not itself free. The tyrant is really dependent on his slaves, and therefore he tries to make them completely useful by making them subservient to his own will. But a lover must have two wills for the realisation of his love, because the consummation of love is in harmony, the harmony between freedom and freedom. So God's love from which our self has taken form has made it separate from God; and it is God's love which again establishes a reconciliation and unites God with our self through the separation. That is why our self has to go through endless renewals. For in its career of separateness it cannot go on for ever. Separateness is the finitude where it finds its barriers to come back again and again to its infinite source. Our self has ceaselessly to cast off its age, repeatedly shed its limits in oblivion and death, in order to realise its immortal youth. Its personality must merge in the universal time after time, in fact pass through it every moment, ever to refresh its individual life. It must follow the eternal rhythm and touch the fundamental unity at every step, and thus maintain its separation balanced in beauty and strength.

The play of life and death we see everywhere—this transmutation of the old into the new. The day comes to us every morning, naked and white, fresh as a flower. But we know it is old. It is age itself. It is that very ancient day which took up the newborn earth in its arms, covered it with its white mantle of light, and sent it forth on its pilgrimage among the stars.

Yet its feet are untired and its eyes undimmed. It carries the golden amulet of ageless eternity, at whose touch all wrinkles vanish from the forehead of creation. In the very core of the world's heart stands immortal youth. Death and decay cast over its face momentary shadows and pass on; they leave no marks of their steps—and truth remains fresh and young.

This old, old day of our earth is born again and again every morning. It comes back to the original refrain of its music. If its march were the march of an infinite straight line, if it had not the awful pause of its plunge in the abysmal darkness and its repeated rebirth in the life of the endless beginning, then it would gradually soil and bury truth with its dust and spread ceaseless aching over the earth under its heavy tread. Then every moment would leave its load of weariness behind, and decrepitude would reign supreme on its throne of eternal dirt.

But every morning the day is reborn among the newly-blossomed flowers with the same message retold and the same assurance renewed that death eternally dies, that the waves of turmoil are on the surface, and that the sea of tranquillity is fathomless. The curtain of night is drawn aside and truth emerges without a speck of dust on its garment, without a furrow of age on its lineaments.

We see that he who is before everything else is the same to-day. Every note of the song of creation comes fresh from his voice. The universe is not a mere echo, reverberating from sky to sky, like a homeless wanderer—the echo of an old song sung once for all in the dim beginning of things and then left orphaned. Every moment it comes from the heart of the master, it is breathed in his breath.

And that is the reason why it overspreads the sky like a thought taking shape in a poem, and never has to break into pieces with the burden of its own accumulating weight. Hence the surprise of endless variations, the advent of the unaccountable, the ceaseless procession of individuals, each of whom is without a parallel in creation. As at the first so to the last, the beginning never ends—the world is ever old and ever new.

It is for our self to know that it must be born anew every moment of its life. It must break through all illusions that encase it in their crust to make it appear old, burdening it with death.

For life is immortal youthfulness, and it hates age that tries to clog its movements—age that belongs not to life in truth, but follows it as the shadow follows the lamp.

Our life, like a river, strikes its banks not to find itself closed in by them, but to realise anew every moment that it has its unending opening towards the sea. It is a poem that strikes its metre at every step not to be silenced by its rigid regulations, but to give expression every moment to the inner freedom of its harmony.

The boundary walls of our individuality thrust us back within our limits, on the one hand, and thus lead us, on the other, to the unlimited. Only when we try to make these limits infinite are we launched into an impossible contradiction and court miserable failure.

This is the cause which leads to the great revolutions in human history. Whenever the part, spurning the whole, tries to run a separate course of its own, the great pull of the all gives it a violent wrench, stops it suddenly, and brings it to the dust. Whenever the individual tries to dam the ever-flowing current of the world-force and imprison it within the area of his particular use, it brings on disaster. However powerful a king may be, he cannot raise his standard or rebellion against the infinite source of strength, which is unity, and yet remain powerful.

It has been said, *By unrighteousness men prosper, gain what they desire, and triumph over their enemies, but at the end they are cut off at the root and suffer extinction.*[38] Our roots must go deep down into the universal if we would attain the greatness of personality.

It is the end of our self to seek that union. It must bend its head low in love and meekness and take its stand where great and small all meet. It has to gain by its loss and rise by its surrender. His games would be a horror to the child if he could not come back to his mother, and our pride of personality will be a curse to us if we cannot give it up in love. We must know that it is only the revelation of the Infinite which is endlessly new and eternally beautiful in us, and which gives the only meaning to our self.

---

38. Adharmēnaidhatē tāvat tatō bahdrāṇi paçyati tatah sapatnān jayati samūlastu vinaçyati.

V

REALISATION IN LOVE

We come now to the eternal problem of co-existence of the infinite and the finite, of the supreme being and our soul. There is a sublime paradox that lies at the root of existence. We never can go round it, because we never can stand outside the problem and weigh it against any other possible alternative. But the problem exists in logic only; in reality it does not offer us any difficulty at all. Logically speaking, the distance between two points, however near, may be said to be infinite because it is infinitely divisible. But we *do* cross the infinite at every step, and meet the eternal in every second. Therefore some of our philosophers say there is no such thing as finitude; it is but a *māyā*, an illusion. The real is the infinite, and it is only *māyā*, the unreality, which causes the appearance of the finite. But the word *māyā* is a mere name, it is no explanation. It is merely saying that with truth there is this appearance which is the opposite of truth; but how they come to exist at one and the same time is incomprehensible.

We have what we call in Sanskrit *dvandva*, a series of opposites in creation; such as, the positive pole and the negative, the centripetal force and the centrifugal, attraction and repulsion. These are also mere names, they are no explanations. They are only different ways of asserting that the world in its essence is a reconciliation of pairs of opposing forces. These forces, like the left and the right hands of the creator, are acting in absolute harmony, yet acting from opposite directions.

There is a bond of harmony between our two eyes, which makes them act in unison. Likewise there is an unbreakable continuity of relation in the physical world between heat and cold, light and darkness, motion and rest, as between the bass and treble notes of a piano. That is why these opposites do not bring confusion in the universe, but harmony. If creation were but a chaos, we should have to imagine the two opposing principles as trying to get the better of each other. But the universe is not under martial law, arbitrary and provisional. Here we find no force which can run amok, or go on indefinitely in its wild road, like an exiled outlaw, breaking all harmony with its surroundings; each force, on the contrary, has to come back in a curved line to its equilibrium. Waves rise, each to its individual height in a seeming attitude of unrelenting competition, but only up to a certain point; and thus we know of the great repose of the sea to which they are all related, and to which they must all return in a rhythm which is marvellously beautiful.

In fact, these undulations and vibrations, these risings and fallings, are not due to the erratic contortions of disparate bodies, they are a rhythmic dance. Rhythm never can be born of the haphazard struggle of combat. Its underlying principle must be unity, not opposition.

This principle of unity is the mystery of all mysteries. The existence of a duality at once raises a question in our minds, and we seek its solution in the One. When at last we find a relation between these two, and thereby see them as one in essence, we feel that we have come to the truth. And then we give utterance to this most startling of all paradoxes, that the One appears as many, that the appearance is the opposite of truth and yet is inseparably related to it.

Curiously enough, there are men who lose that feeling of mystery, which is at the root of all our delights, when they discover the uniformity of law among the diversity of nature.

As if gravitation is not more of a mystery than the fall of an apple, as if the evolution from one scale of being to the other is not something which is even more shy of explanation than a succession of creations. The trouble is that we very often stop at such a law as if it were the final end of our search, and then we find that it does not even begin to emancipate our spirit. It only gives satisfaction to our intellect, and as it does not appeal to our whole being it only deadens in us the sense of the infinite.

A great poem, when analysed, is a set of detached sounds. The reader who finds out the meaning, which is the inner medium that connects these outer sounds, discovers a perfect law all through, which is never violated in the least; the law of the evolution of ideas, the law of the music and the form.

But law in itself is a limit. It only shows that whatever is can never be otherwise. When a man is exclusively occupied with the search for the links of causality, his mind succumbs to the tyranny of law in escaping from the tyranny of facts. In learning a language, when from mere words we reach the laws of words we have gained a great deal. But if we stop at that point, and only concern ourselves with the marvels of the formation of a language, seeking the hidden reason of all its apparent caprices, we do not reach the end–for grammar is not literature, prosody is not a poem.

When we come to literature we find that though it conforms to rules of grammar it is yet a thing of joy, it is freedom itself. The beauty of a poem is bound by strict laws, yet it transcends them. The laws are its wings, they do not keep it weighed down, they carry it to freedom. Its form is in law but its spirit is in beauty. Law is the first step towards freedom, and beauty is the complete liberation which stands on the pedestal of law. Beauty harmonises in itself the limit and the beyond, the law and the liberty.

In the world-poem, the discovery of the law of its rhythms, the measurement of its expansion and contraction, movement and pause, the pursuit of its evolution of forms and characters, are true achievements of the mind; but we cannot stop there. It is like a railway station; but the station platform is not our home. Only he has attained the final truth who knows that the whole world is a creation of joy.

This leads me to think how mysterious the relation of the human heart with nature must be. In the outer world of activity nature has one aspect, but in our hearts, in the inner world, it presents an altogether different picture.

Take an instance—the flower of a plant. However fine and dainty it may look, it is pressed to do a great service, and its colours and forms are all suited to its work. It must bring forth the fruit, or the continuity of plant life will be broken and the earth will be turned into a desert ere long. The colour and the smell of the flower are all for some purpose therefore; no sooner is it fertilised by the bee, and the time of its fruition arrives, than it sheds its exquisite petals and a cruel economy compels it to give up its sweet perfume. It has no time to flaunt its finery, for it is busy beyond measure. Viewed from without, necessity seems to be the only factor in nature for which everything works and moves. There the bud develops into the flower, the flower into the fruit, the fruit into the seed, the seed into a new plant again, and so forth, the chain of activity running on unbroken. Should there crop up any disturbance or impediment, no excuse would be accepted, and the unfortunate thing thus choked in its movement would at once be labelled as rejected, and be bound to die and disappear post-haste. In the great office of nature there are innumerable departments with endless work going on, and the fine flower that you behold there, gaudily attired and scented like a dandy, is by no means what it appears to be, but rather, is like a labourer toiling in sun and shower, who has to submit a clear account of his work and has no breathing space to enjoy himself in playful frolic.

But when this same flower enters the heart of men its aspect of busy practicality is gone, and it becomes the very emblem of leisure and repose. The same object that is the embodiment of endless activity without is the perfect expression of beauty and peace within.

Science here warns us that we are mistaken, that the purpose of a flower is nothing but what is outwardly manifested, and that the relation of beauty and sweetness which we think it bears to us is all our own making, gratuitous and imaginary.

But our heart replies that we are not in the least mistaken. In the sphere of nature the flower carries with it a certificate which recommends it as having immense capacity for doing useful work, but it brings an altogether different letter of introduction when it knocks at the door of our hearts. Beauty becomes its only qualification. At one place it comes as a slave, and at another as a free thing. How, then, should we give credit to its first recommendation and disbelieve the second one? That the flower has got its being in the unbroken chain of causation is true beyond doubt; but that is an outer truth. The inner truth is: *Verily from the everlasting joy do all objects have their birth*[39].

A flower, therefore, has not its only function in nature, but has another great function to exercise in the mind of man. And what is that function? In nature its work is that of a servant who has to make his appearance at appointed times, but in the heart of man it comes like a messenger from the King. In the *Rāmāyana*, when *Sītā*, forcibly separated from her husband, was bewailing her evil fate in *Ravana*'sgolden palace, she was met by a messenger who brought with him a

39. Ānandādhyēva khalvimāni bhūtāni jāyantē.

ring of her beloved *Rāmachandra* himself. The very sight of it convinced *Sītā* of the truth of tidings he bore. She was at once reassured that he came indeed from her beloved one, who had not forgotten her and was at hand to rescue her.

Such a messenger is a flower from our great lover. Surrounded with the pomp and pageantry of worldliness, which may be linked to Ravana's golden city, we still live in exile, while the insolent spirit of worldly prosperity tempts us with allurements and claims us as its bride. In the meantime the flower comes across with a message from the other shore, and whispers in our ears, "I am come. He has sent me. I am a messenger of the beautiful, the one whose soul is the bliss of love. This island of isolation has been bridged over by him, and he has not forgotten thee, and will rescue thee even now. He will draw thee unto him and make thee his own. This illusion will not hold thee in thraldom for ever."

If we happen to be awake then, we question him: "How are we to know that thou art come from him indeed?" The messenger says, "Look! I have this ring from him. How lovely are its hues and charms!"

Ah, doubtless it is his–indeed, it is our wedding ring. Now all else passes into oblivion, only this sweet symbol of the touch of the eternal love fills us with a deep longing. We realise that the palace of gold where we are has nothing to do with us–our deliverance is outside it–and there our love has its fruition and our life its fulfilment.

What to the bee in nature is merely colour and scent, and the marks or spots which show the right track to the honey, is to the human heart beauty and joy untrammelled by necessity. They bring a love letter to the heart written in many-coloured inks.

I was telling you, therefore, that however busy our active nature outwardly may be, she has a secret chamber within the heart where she comes and goes freely, without any design whatsoever. There the fire of her workshop is transformed into lamps of a festival, the noise of her factory is heard like music. The iron chain of cause and effect sounds heavily outside in nature, but in the human heart its unalloyed delight seems to sound, as it were, like the golden strings of a harp.

It indeed seems to be wonderful that nature has these two aspects at one and the same time, and so antithetical—one being of thraldom and the other of freedom. In the same form, sound, colour, and taste two contrary notes are heard, one of necessity and the other of joy. Outwardly nature is busy and restless, inwardly she is all silence and peace. She has toil on one side and leisure on the other. You see her bondage only when you see her from without, but within her heart is a limitless beauty.

Our seer says, "From joy are born all creatures, by joy they are sustained, towards joy they progress, and into joy they enter."

Not that he ignores law, or that his contemplation of this infinite joy is born of the intoxication produced by an indulgence in abstract thought. He fully recognises the inexorable laws of nature, and says, "Fire burns for fear of him (i.e. by his law); the sun shines by fear of him; and for fear of him the wind, the clouds, and death perform their offices." It is a reign of iron rule, ready to punish the least transgression. Yet the poet chants the glad song, "From joy are born all creatures, by joy they are sustained, towards joy they progress, and into joy they enter."

The immortal being manifests himself in joy-form.[40] His manifestation in creation is out of his fullness of joy. It is the nature of this abounding joy to realise itself in form which is law. The joy, which is without form, must create, must translate itself into forms. The joy of the singer is expressed in the form of a song, that of the poet in the form of a poem. Man in his rôle of a creator is ever creating forms, and they come out of his abounding joy.

This joy, whose other name is love, must by its very nature have duality for its realisation. When the singer has his inspiration he makes himself into two; he has within him his other self as the hearer, and the outside audience is merely an extension of this other self of his. The lover seeks his own other self in his beloved. It is the joy that creates this separation, in order to realise through obstacles of union.

The *amritam*, the immortal bliss, has made himself into two. Our soul is the loved one, it is his other self. We are separate; but if this separation were absolute, then there would have been absolute misery and unmitigated evil in this world. Then from untruth we never could reach truth, and from sin we never could hope to attain purity of heart; then all opposites would ever remain opposites, and we could never find a medium through which our differences could ever tend to meet. Then we could have no language, no understanding, no blending of hearts, no co-operation in life. But on the contrary, we find that the separateness of objects is in a fluid state. Their individualities are even changing, they are meeting and merging into each other, till science itself is turning into metaphysics, matter losing its boundaries, and the definition of life becoming more and more indefinite.

Yes, our individual soul has been separated from the supreme soul, but this has not been from alienation but from the

40. Ānandarūpamamritam yad vibhāti.

fullness of love. It is for that reason that untruths, sufferings, and evils are not at a standstill; the human soul can defy them, can overcome them, nay, can altogether transform them into new power and beauty.

The singer is translating his song into singing, his joy into forms, and the hearer has to translate back the singing into the original joy; then the communion between the singer and the hearer is complete. The infinite joy is manifesting itself in manifold forms, taking upon itself the bondage of law, and we fulfil our destiny when we go back from forms to joy, from law to the love, when we untie the knot of the finite and hark back to the infinite.

The human soul is on its journey from the law to love, from discipline to liberation, from the moral plane to the spiritual. Buddha preached the discipline of self-restraint and moral life; it is a complete acceptance of law. But this bondage of law cannot be an end by itself; by mastering it thoroughly we acquire the means of getting beyond it. It is going back to Brahma, to the infinite love, which is manifesting itself through the finite forms of law. Buddha names it *Brahma-vihāra*, the joy of living in Brahma. He who wants to reach this stage, according to Buddha, "shall deceive none, entertain no hatred for anybody, and never wish to injure through anger. He shall have measureless love for all creatures, even as a mother has for her only child, whom she protects with her own life. Up above, below, and all around him he shall extend his love, which is without bounds and obstacles, and which is free from all cruelty and antagonism. While standing, sitting, walking, lying down, till he fall asleep, he shall keep his mind active in this exercise of universal goodwill."

Want of love is a degree of callousness; for love is the perfection of consciousness. We do not love because we do not comprehend, or rather we do not comprehend because we do not love. For love is the ultimate meaning of everything around us. It is not a mere sentiment; it is truth; it is the joy that is at the root of all creation. It is the white light of pure consciousness that emanates from Brahma. So, to be one with this *sarvānubhūh*, this all-feeling being who is in the external sky, as well as in our inner soul, we must attain to that summit of consciousness, which is love: *Who could have breathed or moved if the sky were not filled with joy, with love?*[41] It is through the heightening of our consciousness into love, and extending it all over the world, that we can attain *Brahma-vihāra*, communion with this infinite joy.

Love spontaneously gives itself in endless gifts. But these gifts lose their fullest significance if through them we do not reach that love, which is the giver. To do that, we must have love in our own heart. He who has no love in him values the gifts of his lover only according to their usefulness. But utility is temporary and partial. It can never occupy our whole being; what is useful only touches us at the point where we have some want. When the want is satisfied, utility becomes a burden if it still persists. On the other hand, a mere token is of permanent worth to us when we have love in our heart. For it is not for any special use. It is an end in itself; it is for our whole being and therefore can never tire us.

The question is, In what manner do we accept this world, which is a perfect gift of joy? Have we been able to receive it in our heart where we keep enshrined things that are of deathless value to us? We are frantically busy making use of the forces of the universe to gain more and more power; we feed and we clothe ourselves from its stores, we scramble for its riches, and it becomes for us a field of fierce competition. But were we born for this, to extend our proprietary rights over this world and make of it a marketable commodity? When our

---

41. Ko hyēvānyāt kah prānyāt yadēsha ākāça ānandō na syāt.

whole mind is bent only upon making use of this world it loses for us its true value. We make it cheap by our sordid desires; and thus to the end of our days we only try to feed upon it and miss its truth, just like the greedy child who tears leaves from a precious book and tries to swallow them.

In the lands where cannibalism is prevalent man looks upon man as his food. In such a country civilisation can never thrive, for there man loses his higher value and is made common indeed. But there are other kinds of cannibalism, perhaps not so gross, but not less heinous, for which one need not travel far. In countries higher in the scale of civilisation we find sometimes man looked upon as a mere body, and he is bought and sold in the market by the price of his flesh only. And sometimes he gets his sole value from being useful; he is made into a machine, and is traded upon by the man of money to acquire for him more money. Thus our lust, our greed, our love of comfort result in cheapening man to his lowest value. It is self deception on a large scale. Our desires blind us to the *truth* that there is in man, and this is the greatest wrong done by ourselves to our own soul. It deadens our consciousness, and is but a gradual method of spiritual suicide. It produces ugly sores in the body of civilisation, gives rise to its hovels and brothels, its vindictive penal codes, its cruel prison systems, its organised method of exploiting foreign races to the extent of permanently injuring them by depriving them of the discipline of self-government and means of self-defence.

Of course man is useful to man, because his body is a marvellous machine and his mind an organ of wonderful efficiency. But he is a spirit as well, and this spirit is truly known only by love. When we define a man by the market value of the service we can expect of him, we know him imperfectly. With this limited knowledge of him it becomes easy for us to be unjust to him and to entertain feelings of triumphant self-congratulation when, on account of some cruel advantage on our side, we can get out of him much more than we have paid for. But when we know him as a spirit we know him as our own. We at once feel that cruelty to him is cruelty to ourselves, to make him small is stealing from our own humanity, and in seeking to make use of him solely for personal profit we merely gain in money or comfort what we pay in truth.

One day I was out in a boat on the Ganges. It was a beautiful evening in autumn. The sun had just set; the silence of the sky was full to the brim with ineffable peace and beauty. The vast expanse of water was without a ripple, mirroring all the changing shades of the sunset glow. Miles and miles of a desolate sandbank lay like a huge amphibious reptile of some antediluvian age, with its scales glistening in shining colours. As our boat was silently gliding by the precipitous river-bank, riddled with the nest-holes of a colony of birds, suddenly a big fish leapt up to the surface of the water and then disappeared, displaying on its vanishing figure all the colours of the evening sky. It drew aside for a moment the many-coloured screen behind which there was a silent world full of the joy of life. It came up from the depths of its mysterious dwelling with a beautiful dancing motion and added its own music to the silent symphony of the dying day. I felt as if I had a friendly greeting from an alien world in its own language, and it touched my heart with a flash of gladness. Then suddenly the man at the helm exclaimed with a distinct note of regret, "Ah, what a big fish!" It at once brought before his vision the picture of the fish caught and made ready for his supper. He could only look at the fish through his desire, and thus missed the whole truth of its existence. But man is not entirely an animal. He aspires to a spiritual vision, which is the vision of the whole truth. This gives him the highest delight, because it reveals to him the deepest harmony that exists between him and his surroundings. It is our desires that limit the scope of our self-realisation, hinder our extension of consciousness, and give rise to sin, which is the innermost barrier that keeps us apart from our God, setting up disunion and the arrogance of exclusiveness. For sin is not one mere action, but it is an attitude of life which takes for granted that our goal is finite, that our self is the ultimate truth, and that we are not all essentially one but exist each for his own separate individual existence.

So I repeat we never can have a true view of man unless we have a love for him. Civilisation must be judged and prized, not by the amount of power it has developed, but by how much it has evolved and given expression to, by its laws and institutions, the love of humanity. The first question and the last which it has to answer is, Whether and how far it recognises man more as a spirit than a machine? Whenever some ancient civilisation fell into decay and died, it was owing to causes which produced callousness of heart and led to the cheapening of man's worth; when either the state or some powerful group of men began to look upon the people as a mere instrument of their power; when, by compelling weaker races to slavery and trying to keep them down by every means, man struck at the foundation of his greatness, his own love of freedom and fair-play. Civilisation can never sustain itself upon cannibalism of any form. For that by which alone man is true can only be nourished by love and justice.

As with man, so with this universe. When we look at the world through the veil of our desires we make it small and narrow, and fail to perceive its full truth. Of course it is obvious that the world serves us and fulfils our needs, but our relation to it does not end there. We are bound to it with a deeper and truer bond than that of necessity. Our soul is drawn to it; our love of life is really our wish to continue our relation with this great world. This relation is one of love. We are glad that we are in it; we are attached to it with numberless threads, which extend from this earth to the stars. Man foolishly tries to prove his superiority by imagining his radical separateness from what he calls his physical world, which, in his blind fanaticism, he sometimes goes to the extent of ignoring altogether, holding it at his direst enemy. Yet the more his knowledge progresses, the more it becomes difficult for man to establish this separateness, and all the imaginary boundaries he had set up around himself vanish one after another. Every time we lose some of our badges of absolute distinction by which we conferred upon our humanity the right to hold itself apart from its surroundings, it gives us a shock of humiliation. But we have to submit to this. If we set up our pride on the path of our self-realisation to create divisions and disunion, then it must sooner or later come under the wheels of truth and be ground to dust. No, we are not burdened with some monstrous superiority, unmeaning in its singular abruptness. It would be utterly degrading for us to live in a world immeasurably less than ourselves in the quality of soul, just as it would be repulsive and degrading to be surrounded and served by a host of slaves, day and night, from birth to the moment of death. On the contrary, this world is our compeer, nay, we are one with it.

Through our progress in science the wholeness of the world and our oneness with it is becoming clearer to our mind. When this perception of the perfection of unity is not merely intellectual, when it opens out our whole being into a luminous consciousness of the all, then it becomes a radiant joy, an overspreading love. Our spirit finds its larger self in the whole world, and is filled with an absolute certainty that it is immortal. It dies a hundred times in its enclosures of self; for separateness is doomed to die, it cannot be made eternal. But it never can die where it is one with the all, for there is its truth, its joy. When a man feels the rhythmic throb of the soul-life of the whole world in his own soul, then is he free. Then he enters into the secret courting that goes on between this beautiful world-bride, veiled with the veil of the many-coloured finiteness, and the *paramatmam*, the bridegroom, in his spotless white. Then he knows that he is the partaker of this gorgeous love festival, and he is the honoured guest at the feast of immortality. Then he understands the meaning of the seer-poet who sings, "From love the world is born, by love it is sustained, towards love it moves, and into love it enters."

In love all the contradictions of existence merge themselves and are lost. Only in love are unity and duality not at variance. Love must be one and two at the same time.

Only love is motion and rest in one. Our heart ever changes its place till it finds love, and then it has its rest. But this rest itself is an intense form of activity where utter quiescence and unceasing energy meet at the same point in love.

In love, loss and gain are harmonised. In its balance-sheet, credit and debit accounts are in the same column, and gifts are added to gains. In this wonderful festival of creation, this great ceremony of self-sacrifice of God, the lover constantly gives himself up to gain himself in love. Indeed, love is what brings together and inseparably connects both the act of abandoning and that of receiving.

In love, at one of its poles you find the personal, and at the other the impersonal. At one you have the positive assertion–Here I am; at the other the equally strong denial–I am not. Without this ego what is love? And again, with only this ego how can love be possible?

Bondage and liberation are not antagonistic in love. For love is most free and at the same time most bound. If God were absolutely free there would be no creation. The infinite being has assumed unto himself the mystery of finitude. And in him who is love the finite and the infinite are made one.

Similarly, when we talk about the relative values of freedom and non-freedom, it becomes a mere play of words. It is not that we desire freedom alone, we want thraldom as well. It is the high function of love to welcome all limitations and to transcend them. For nothing is more independent than love, and where else, again, shall we find so much of dependence? In love, thraldom is as glorious as freedom.

The *Vaishnava* religion has boldly declared that God has bound himself to man, and in that consists the greatest glory of human existence. In the spell of the wonderful rhythm of the finite he fetters himself at every step, and thus gives his love out in music in his most perfect lyrics of beauty. Beauty is his wooing of our heart; it can have no other purpose. It tells us everywhere that the display of power is not the ultimate meaning of creation; wherever there is a bit of colour, a note of song, a grace of form, there comes the call for our love. Hunger compels us to obey its behests, but hunger is not the last word for a man. There have been men who have deliberately defied its commands to show that the human soul is not to be led by the pressure of wants and threat of pain. In fact, to live the life of man we have to resist its demands every day, the least of us as well as the greatest. But, on the other hand, there is a beauty in the world which never insults our freedom, never raises even its little finger to make us acknowledge its sovereignty. We can absolutely ignore it and suffer no penalty in consequence. It is a call to us, but not a command. It seeks for love in us, and love can never be had by compulsion. Compulsion is not indeed the final appeal to man, but joy is. Any joy is everywhere; it is in the earth's green covering of grass; in the blue serenity of the sky; in the reckless exuberance of spring; in the severe abstinence of grey winter; in the living flesh that animates our bodily frame; in the perfect poise of the human figure, noble and upright; in living; in the exercise of all our powers; in the acquisition of knowledge; in fighting evils; in dying for gains we never can share. Joy is there everywhere; it is superfluous, unnecessary; nay, it very often contradicts the most peremptory behests of necessity. It exists to show that the bonds of law can only be explained by love; they are like body and soul. Joy is the realisation of the truth of oneness, the oneness of our soul with the world and of the world-soul with the supreme lover.

VI

REALISATION IN ACTION

It is only those who have known that joy expresses itself through law who have learnt to transcend the law. Not that the bonds of law have ceased to exist for them—but that the bonds have become to them as the form of freedom incarnate. The freed soul delights in accepting bonds, and does not seek to evade any of them, for in each does it feel the manifestation of an infinite energy whose joy is in creation.

As a matter of fact, where there are no bonds, where there is the madness of license, the soul ceases to be free. There is its hurt; there is its separation from the infinite, its agony of sin. Whenever at the call of temptation the soul falls away from the bondage of law, then, like a child deprived of the support of its mother's arms, it cries out, *Smite me not!*[42] "Bind me," it prays, "oh, bind me in the bonds of thy law; bind me within and without; hold me tight; let me in the clasp of thy law be bound up together with thy joy; protect me by thy firm hold from the deadly laxity of sin."

As some, under the idea that law is the opposite of joy, mistake intoxication for joy, so there are many in our country who imagine action to be opposed to freedom. They think that activity being in the material plane is a restriction of the free spirit of the soul. But we must remember that as joy expresses itself in law, so the soul finds its freedom in action. It is because

42. Mā mā himsīh.

joy cannot find expression in itself alone that it desires the law which is outside. Likewise it is because the soul cannot find freedom within itself that it wants external action. The soul of man is ever freeing itself from its own folds by its activity; had it been otherwise it could not have done any voluntary work.

The more man acts and makes actual what was latent in him, the nearer does he bring the distant Yet-to-be. In that actualisation man is ever making himself more and yet more distinct, and seeing himself clearly under newer and newer aspects in the midst of his varied activities, in the state, in society. This vision makes for freedom.

Freedom is not in darkness, nor in vagueness. There is no bondage so fearful as that of obscurity. It is to escape from this obscurity that the seed struggles to sprout, the bud to blossom. It is to rid itself of this envelope of vagueness that the ideas in our mind are constantly seeking opportunities to take on outward form. In the same way our soul, in order to release itself from the mist of indistinctness and come out into the open, is continually creating for itself fresh fields of action, and is busy contriving new forms of activity, even such as are not needful for the purposes of its earthly life. And why? Because it wants freedom. It wants to see itself, to realise itself.

When man cuts down the pestilential jungle and makes unto himself a garden, the beauty that he thus sets free from within its enclosure of ugliness is the beauty of his own soul: without giving it this freedom outside, he cannot make it free within. When he implants law and order in the midst of the waywardness of society, the good which he sets free from the obstruction of the bad is the goodness of his own soul: without being thus made free outside it cannot find freedom within. Thus is man continually engaged in setting free in action his powers, his beauty, his goodness, his very soul. And the more he succeeds in so doing, the greater does he see himself to be, the broader becomes the field of his knowledge of self.

The Upanishad says: *In the midst of activity alone wilt thou desire to live a hundred years.*[43] It is the saying of those who had amply tasted of the joy of the soul. Those who have fully realised the soul have never talked in mournful accents of the sorrowfulness of life or of the bondage of action. They are not like the weakling flower whose stem-hold is so light that it drops away before attaining fruition. They hold on to life with all their might and say, "never will we let go till the fruit is ripe." They desire in their joy to express themselves strenuously in their life and in their work. Pain and sorrow dismay them not, they are not bowed down to the dust by the weight of their own heart. With the erect head of the victorious hero they march through life seeing themselves and showing themselves in increasing resplendence of soul through both joys and sorrows. The joy of their life keeps step with the joy of that energy which is playing at building and breaking throughout the universe. The joy of the sunlight, the joy of the free air, mingling with the joy of their lives, makes one sweet harmony reign within and without. It is they who say, *In the midst of activity alone wilt thou desire to live a hundred years.*

This joy of life, this joy of work, in man is absolutely true. It is no use saying that it is a delusion of ours; that unless we cast it away we cannot enter upon the path of self-realisation. It will never do the least good to attempt the realisation of the infinite apart from the world of action.

It is not the truth that man is active on compulsion. If there is compulsion on one side, on the other there is pleasure; on the one hand action is spurred on by want, on the other it hies to its natural fulfilment. That is why, as man's civilisation advances, he increases his obligations and the work that he

43. Kurvannēvēha karmāni jijīvishet çatam samāh.

willingly creates for himself. One should have thought that nature had given him quite enough to do to keep him busy, in fact that it was working him to death with the lash of hunger and thirst,–but no. Man does not think that sufficient; he cannot rest content with only doing the work that nature prescribes for him in common with the birds and beasts. He needs must surpass all, even in activity. No creature has to work so hard as man; he has been impelled to contrive for himself a vast field of action in society; and in this field he is for every building up and pulling down, making and unmaking laws, piling up heaps of material, and incessantly thinking, seeking and suffering. In this field he has fought his mightiest battles, gained continual new life, made death glorious, and, far from evading troubles, has willingly and continually taken up the burden of fresh trouble. He has discovered the truth that he is not complete in the cage of his immediate surroundings, that he is greater than his present, and that while to stand still in one place may be comforting, the arrest of life destroys his true function and the real purpose of his existence.

This *mahatī vinashtih–this great destruction* he cannot bear, and accordingly he toils and suffers in order that he may gain in stature by transcending his present, in order to become that which he yet is not. In this travail is man's glory, and it is because he knows it, that he has not sought to circumscribe his field of action, but is constantly occupied in extending the bounds. Sometimes he wanders so far that his work tends to lose its meaning, and his rushings to and fro create fearful eddies round different centres–eddies of self-interest, of pride of power. Still, so long as the strength of the current is not lost, there is no fear; the obstructions and the dead accumulations of his activity are dissipated and carried away; the impetus corrects its own mistakes. Only when the soul sleeps in stagnation do its enemies gain overmastering strength, and these obstructions become too clogging to be fought through. Hence have we been warned by our teachers that to work we must live, to live we must work; that life and activity are inseparably connected.

It is very characteristic of life that it is not complete within itself; it must come out. Its truth is in the commerce of the inside and the outside. In order to live, the body must maintain its various relations with the outside light and air—not only to gain life-force, but also to manifest it. Consider how fully employed the body is with its own inside activities; its heartbeat must not stop for a second, its stomach, its brain, must be ceaselessly working. Yet this is not enough; the body is outwardly restless all the while. Its life leads it to an endless dance of work and play outside; it cannot be satisfied with the circulations of its internal economy, and only finds the fulfilment of joy in its outward excursions.

The same with the soul. It cannot live on its own internal feelings and imaginings. It is ever in need of external objects; not only to feed its inner consciousness but to apply itself in action, not only to receive but also to give.

The real truth is, we cannot live if we divide him who is truth itself into two parts. We must abide in him within as well as without. In whichever aspect we deny him we deceive ourselves and incur a loss.*Brahma has not left me, let me not leave Brahma.*[44] If we say that we would realise him in introspection alone and leave him out of our external activity, that we would enjoy him by the love in our heart, but not worship him by outward ministrations; or if we say the opposite, and overweight ourselves on one side in the journey of our life's quest, we shall alike totter to our downfall.

In the great western continent we see that the soul of man is mainly concerned with extending itself outwards; the

44. Māham brahma nirākuryyām mā mā brahma nirākarōt.

open field of the exercise of power is its field. Its partiality is entirely for the world of extension, and it would leave aside–nay, hardly believe in–that field of inner consciousness which is the field of fulfilment. It has gone so far in this that the perfection of fulfilment seems to exist for it nowhere. Its science has always talked of the never-ending evolution of the world. Its metaphysic has now begun to talk of the evolution of God himself. They will not admit that he *is*; they would have it that he also is *becoming*.

They fail to realise that while the infinite is always greater than any assignable limit, it is also complete; that on the one hand Brahma is evolving, on the other he is perfection; that in the one aspect he is essence, in the other manifestation–both together at the same time, as is the song and the act of singing. This is like ignoring the consciousness of the singer and saying that only the singing is in progress, that there is no song. Doubtless we are directly aware only of the singing, and never at any one time of the song as a whole; but do we not all the time know that the complete song is in the soul of the singer?

It is because of this insistence on the doing and the becoming that we perceive in the west the intoxication of power. These men seem to have determined to despoil and grasp everything by force. They would always obstinately be doing and never be done–they would not allow to death its natural place in the scheme of things–they know not the beauty of completion.

In our country the danger comes from the opposite side. Our partiality is for the internal world. We would cast aside with contumely the field of power and of extension. We would realise Brahma in mediation only in his aspect of completeness, we have determined not to see him in the commerce of the universe in his aspect of evolution. That is why in our seekers we so often find the intoxication of the spirit and its consequent degradation. Their faith would acknowledge no bondage of law, their imagination soars unrestricted, their conduct disdains to offer any explanation to reason. Their intellect, in its vain attempts to see Brahma inseparable from his creation, works itself stone-dry, and their heart, seeking to confine him within its own outpourings, swoons in a drunken ecstasy of emotion. They have not even kept within reach any standard whereby they can measure the loss of strength and character which manhood sustains by thus ignoring the bonds of law and the claims of action in the external universe.

But true spirituality, as taught in our sacred lore, is calmly balanced in strength, in the correlation of the within and the without. The truth has its law, it has its joy. On one side of it is being chanted the *Bhayādasyāgnistapati*[45], on the other the *Ānandādhyeva khalvimāni bhūtāni jāyante.*[46] Freedom is impossible of attainment without submission to law, for Brahma is in one aspect bound by his truth, in the other free in his joy.

As for ourselves, it is only when we wholly submit to the bonds of truth that we fully gain the joy of freedom. And how? As does the string that is bound to the harp. When the harp is truly strung, when there is not the slightest laxity in the strength of the bond, then only does music result; and the string transcending itself in its melody finds at every chord its true freedom. It is because it is bound by such hard and fast rules on the one side that it can find this range of freedom in music on the other. While the string was not true, it was indeed merely bound; but a loosening of its bondage would not have been the way to freedom, which it can only fully achieve by being bound tighter and tighter till it has attained the true pitch.

---

45. "For fear of him the fire doth burn," etc

46. "From Joy are born all created things," etc.

The bass and treble strings of our duty are only bonds so long as we cannot maintain them steadfastly attuned according to the law of truth; and we cannot call by the name of freedom the loosening of them into the nothingness of inaction. That is why I would say that the true striving in the quest of truth, of *dharma*, consists not in the neglect of action but in the effort to attune it closer and closer to the eternal harmony. The text of this striving should be, *Whatever works thou doest, consecrate them to Brahma.*[47] That is to say, the soul is to dedicate itself to Brahma through all its activities. This dedication is the song of the soul, in this is its freedom. Joy reigns when all work becomes the path to the union with Brahma; when the soul ceases to return constantly to its own desires; when in it our self-offering grows more and more intense. Then there is completion, then there is freedom, then, in this world, comes the kingdom of God.

Who is there that, sitting in his corner, would deride this grand self-expression of humanity in action, this incessant self-consecration? Who is there that thinks the union of God and man is to be found in some secluded enjoyment of his own imaginings, away from the sky-towering temple of the greatness of humanity, which the whole of mankind, in sunshine and storm, is toiling to erect through the ages? Who is there that thinks this secluded communion is the highest form of religion?

O thou distraught wanderer, thou *Sannyasin*, drunk in the wine of self-intoxication, dost thou not already hear the progress of the human soul along the highway traversing the wide fields of humanity–the thunder of its progress in the car of its achievements, which is destined to overpass the bounds that prevent its expansion into the universe? The very mountains are cleft asunder and give way before the march of its ban-

---

47. Yadyat karma prakurvīta tadbrahmani samarpayet.

ners waving triumphantly in the heavens; as the mist before the rising sun, the tangled obscurities of material things vanish at its irresistible approach. Pain, disease, and disorder are at every step receding before its onset; the obstructions of ignorance are being thrust aside; the darkness of blindness is being pierced through; and behold, the promised land of wealth and health, of poetry and art, of knowledge and righteousness is gradually being revealed to view. Do you in your lethargy desire to say that this car of humanity, which is shaking the very earth with the triumph of its progress along the mighty vistas of history, has no charioteer leading it on to its fulfilment? Who is there who refuses to respond to his call to join in this triumphal progress? Who so foolish as to run away from the gladsome throng and seek him in the listlessness of inaction? Who so steeped in untruth as to dare to call all this untrue—this great world of men, this civilisation of expanding humanity, this eternal effort of man, through depths of sorrow, through heights of gladness, through innumerable impediments within and without, to win victory for his powers? He who can think of this immensity of achievement as an immense fraud, can he truly believe in God who is the truth? He who thinks to reach God by running away from the world, when and where does he expect to meet him? How far can he fly—can he fly and fly, till he flies into nothingness itself? No, the coward who would fly can nowhere find him. We must be brave enough to be able to say: We are reaching him here in this very spot, now at this very moment. We must be able to assure ourselves that as in our actions we are realising ourselves, so in ourselves we are realising him who is the self of self. We must earn the right to say so unhesitatingly by clearing away with our own effort all obstruction, all disorder, all discords from our path of activity; we must be able to say, "In my work is my joy, and in that joy does the joy of my joy abide."

Whom does the Upanishad call *The chief among the knowers of Brahma?*[48] He is defined as *He whose joy is in Brahma, whose play is in Brahma, the active one.*[49] Joy without the play of joy is no joy at all—play without activity is no play. Activity is the play of joy. He whose joy is in Brahma, how can he live in inaction? For must he not by his activity provide that in which the joy of Brahma is to take form and manifest itself? That is why he who knows Brahma, who has his joy in Brahma, must also have all his activity in Brahma—his eating and drinking, his earning of livelihood and his beneficence. Just as the joy of the poet in his poem, of the artist in his art, of the brave man in the output of his courage, of the wise man in his discernment of truths, ever seeks expression in their several activities, so the joy of the knower of Brahma, in the whole of his everyday work, little and big, in truth, in beauty, in orderliness and in beneficence, seeks to give expression to the infinite.

Brahma himself gives expression to his joy in just the same way. *By his many-sided activity, which radiates in all directions, does he fulfil the inherent want of his different creatures.*[50] That inherent want is he himself, and so he is in so many ways, in so many forms, giving himself. He works, for without working how could he give himself. His joy is ever dedicating itself in the dedication which is his creation.

In this very thing does our own true meaning lie, in this is our likeness to our father. We must also give up ourselves in many-sided variously aimed activity. In the Vedas he is called *the giver of himself, the giver of strength.*[51] He is not content with giving us himself, but he gives us strength that we may likewise give ourselves. That is why the seer of the Upanishad prays to him who is thus fulfilling our wants, *May*

48. Brahmavidāmvaristhah.
49. Ātmakrīrha ātmaratih kriyāvān.
50. Bahudhā çakti yogāt varṇānanekān nihitārtho dadhāti.
51. Ātmadā baladā.

he grant us the beneficent mind[52], may he fulfil that uttermost want of ours by granting us the beneficent mind. That is to say, it is not enough he should alone work to remove our want, but he should give us the desire and the strength to work with him in his activity and in the exercise of the goodness. Then, indeed, will our union with him alone be accomplished. The beneficent mind is that which shows us the want (*swārtha*) of another self to be the inherent want (*nihitārtha*) of our own self; that which shows that our joy consists in the varied aiming of our many-sided powers in the work of humanity. When we work under the guidance of this beneficent mind, then our activity is regulated, but does not become mechanical; it is action not goaded on by want, but stimulated by the satisfaction of the soul. Such activity ceases to be a blind imitation of that of the multitude, a cowardly following of the dictates of fashion. Therein we begin to see that *He is in the beginning and in the end of the universe*[53], and likewise see that of our own work is he the fount and the inspiration, and at the end thereof is he, and therefore that all our activity is pervaded by peace and good and joy.

The Upanishad says: *Knowledge, power, and action are of his nature.*[54] It is because this naturalness has not yet been born in us that we tend to divide joy from work. Our day of work is not our day of joy–for that we require a holiday; for, miserable that we are, we cannot find our holiday in our work. The river finds its holiday in its onward flow, the fire in its outburst of flame, the scent of the flower in its permeation of the atmosphere; but in our everyday work there is no such holiday for us. It is because we do not let ourselves go, because we do not give ourselves joyously and entirely up to it, that our work overpowers us.

---

52. Sa no buddhya çubhayā samyunaktu.
53. Vichaiti chāntē viçvamādau.
54. Svābhāvikījnāna bala kriyā cha.

O giver of thyself! at the vision of thee as joy let our souls flame up to thee as the fire, flow on to thee as the river, permeate thy being as the fragrance of the flower. Give us strength to love, to love fully, our life in its joys and sorrows, in its gains and losses, in its rise and fall. Let us have strength enough fully to see and hear thy universe, and to work with full vigour therein. Let us fully live the life thou hast given us, let us bravely take and bravely give. This is our prayer to thee. Let us once for all dislodge from our minds the feeble fancy that would make out thy joy to be a thing apart from action, thin, formless, and unsustained. Wherever the peasant tills the hard earth, there does thy joy gush out in the green of the corn, wherever man displaces the entangled forest, smooths the stony ground, and clears for himself a homestead, there does thy joy enfold it in orderliness and peace.

O worker of the universe! We would pray to thee to let the irresistible current of thy universal energy come like the impetuous south wind of spring, let it come rushing over the vast field of the life of man, let it bring the scent of many flowers, the murmurings of many woodlands, let it make sweet and vocal the lifelessness of our dried-up soul-life. Let our newly awakened powers cry out for unlimited fulfilment in leaf and flower and fruit.

VII

THE REALISATION OF BEAUTY

Things in which we do not take joy are either a burden upon our minds to be got rid of at any cost; or they are useful, and therefore in temporary and partial relation to us, becoming burdensome when their utility is lost; or they are like wandering vagabonds, loitering for a moment on the outskirts of our recognition, and then passing on. A thing is only completely our own when it is a thing of joy to us.

The greater part of this world is to us as if it were nothing. But we cannot allow it to remain so, for thus it belittles our own self. The entire world is given to us, and all our powers have their final meaning in the faith that by their help we are to take possession of our patrimony.

But what is the function of our sense of beauty in this process of the extension of our consciousness? Is it there to separate truth into strong lights and shadows, and bring it before us in its uncompromising distinction of beauty and ugliness? If that were so, then we would have had to admit that this sense of beauty creates a dissension in our universe and sets up a wall of hindrance across the highway of communication that leads from everything to all things.

But that cannot be true. As long as our realisation is incomplete a division necessarily remains between things known and unknown, pleasant and unpleasant. But in spite of the dictum of some philosophers man does not accept any arbitrary and absolute limit to his knowable world. Every day his science is penetrating into the region formerly marked in his map as unexplored or inexplorable. Our sense of beauty is similarly engaged in ever pushing on its conquests. Truth is everywhere, therefore everything is the object of our knowledge. Beauty is omnipresent, therefore everything is capable of giving us joy.

In the early days of his history man took everything as a phenomenon of life. His science of life began by creating a sharp distinction between life and non-life. But as it is proceeding farther and farther the line of demarcation between the animate and inanimate is growing more and more dim. In the beginning of our apprehension these sharp lines of contrast are helpful to us, but as our comprehension becomes clearer they gradually fade away.

The Upanishads have said that all things are created and sustained by an infinite joy. To realise this principle of creation we have to start with a division–the division into the beautiful and the non-beautiful. Then the apprehension of beauty has to come to us with a vigorous blow to awaken our consciousness from its primitive lethargy, and it attains its object by the urgency of the contrast. Therefore our first acquaintance with beauty is in her dress of motley colours, that affects us with its stripes and feathers, nay, with its disfigurements. But as our acquaintance ripens, the apparent discords are resolved into modulations of rhythm. At first we detach beauty from its surroundings, we hold it apart from the rest, but at the end we realise its harmony with all. Then the music of beauty has no more need of exciting us with loud noise; it renounces violence, and appeals to our heart with the truth that it is meekness inherits the earth.

In some stage of our growth, in some period of our history, we try to set up a special cult of beauty, and pare it down to a narrow circuit, so as to make it a matter of pride for a chosen few. Then it breeds in its votaries affections and exaggerations, as it did with the Brahmins in the time of the decadence of Indian civilisation, when the perception of the higher truth fell away and superstitions grew up unchecked.

In the history of æsthetics there also comes an age of emancipation when the recognition of beauty in things great and small become easy, and when we see it more in the unassuming harmony of common objects than in things startling in their singularity. So much so, that we have to go through the stages of reaction when in the representation of beauty we try to avoid everything that is obviously pleasing and that has been crowned by the sanction of convention. We are then tempted in defiance to exaggerate the commonness of commonplace things, thereby making them aggressively uncommon. To restore harmony we create the discords which are a feature of all reactions. We already see in the present age the sign of this æsthetic reaction, which proves that man has at last come to know that it is only the narrowness of perception which sharply divides the field of his æsthetic consciousness into ugliness and beauty. When he has the power to see things detached from self-interest and from the insistent claims of the lust of the senses, then alone can he have the true vision of the beauty that is everywhere. Then only can he see that what is unpleasant to us is not necessarily unbeautiful, but has its beauty in truth.

When we say that beauty is everywhere we do not mean that the word ugliness should be abolished from our language, just as it would be absurd to say that there is no such thing as untruth. Untruth there certainly is, not in the system of the universe, but in our power of comprehension, as its negative element. In the same manner there is ugliness in the distorted expression of beauty in our life and in our art which comes from our imperfect realisation of Truth. To a certain extent we can set our life against the law of truth which is in us and which is in all, and likewise we can give rise to ugliness by going counter to the eternal law of harmony which is everywhere.

Through our sense of truth we realise law in creation, and through our sense of beauty we realise harmony in the universe. When we recognise the law in nature we extend our mastery over physical forces and become powerful; when we recognise the law in our moral nature we attain mastery over self and become free. In like manner the more we comprehend the harmony in the physical world the more our life shares the gladness of creation, and our expression of beauty in art becomes more truly catholic. As we become conscious of the harmony in our soul, our apprehension of the blissfulness of the spirit of the world becomes universal, and the expression of beauty in our life moves in goodness and love towards the infinite. This is the ultimate object of our existence, that we must ever know that "beauty is truth, truth beauty"; we must realise the whole world in love, for love gives it birth, sustains it, and takes it back to its bosom. We must have that perfect emancipation of heart which gives us the power to stand at the innermost centre of things and have the taste of that fullness of disinterested joy which belongs to Brahma.

Music is the purest form of art, and therefore the most direct expression of beauty, with a form and spirit which is one and simple, and least encumbered with anything extraneous. We seem to feel that the manifestation of the infinite in the finite forms of creation is music itself, silent and visible. The evening sky, tirelessly repeating the starry constellations, seems like a child struck with wonder at the mystery of its own first utterance, lisping the same word over and over again, and listening to it in unceasing joy. When in the rainy night of July the darkness is thick upon the meadows and the pattering rain draws veil upon veil over the stillness of the slumbering earth, this monotony of the rain patter seems to be the darkness of sound itself. The gloom of the dim and dense line of trees, the thorny bushes scattered in the bare heath like floating heads of swimmers with bedraggled hair, the smell of the damp grass and the wet earth, the spire of the temple rising above the undefined mass of blackness grouped around the village huts–everything seems like notes rising from the heart of the night, mingling and losing themselves in the one sound of ceaseless rain filling the sky.

Therefore the true poets, they who are seers, seek to express the universe in terms of music.

They rarely use symbols of painting to express the unfolding of forms, the mingling of endless lines and colours that goes on every moment on the canvas of the blue sky.

They have their reason. For the man who paints must have canvas, brush and colour-box. The first touch of his brush is very far from the complete idea. And then when the work is finished the artist is gone, the windowed picture stands alone, the incessant touches of love of the creative hand are withdrawn.

But the singer has everything within him. The notes come out from his very life. They are not materials gathered from outside. His idea and his expression are brother and sister; very often they are born as twins. In music the heart reveals itself immediately; it suffers not from any barrier of alien material.

Therefore though music has to wait for its completeness like any other art, yet at every step it gives out the beauty of the whole. As the material of expression even words are barriers, for their meaning has to be constructed by thought. But music never has to depend upon any obvious meaning; it expresses what no words can ever express.

What is more, music and the musician are inseparable. When the singer departs, his singing dies with him; it is in eternal union with the life and joy of the master.

This world-song is never for a moment separated from its singer. It is not fashioned from any outward material. It is his joy itself taking never-ending form. It is the great heart sending the tremor of its thrill over the sky.

There is a perfection in each individual strain of this music, which is the revelation of completion in the incomplete. No one of its notes is final, yet each reflects the infinite.

What does it matter if we fail to derive the exact meaning of this great harmony? Is it not like the hand meeting the string and drawing out at once all its tones at the touch? It is the language of beauty, the caress, that comes from the heart of the world straightway reaches our heart.

Last night, in the silence which pervaded the darkness, I stood alone and heard the voice of the singer of eternal melodies. When I went to sleep I closed my eyes with this last thought in my mind, that even when I remain unconscious in slumber the dance of life will still go on in the hushed arena of my sleeping body, keeping step with the stars. The heart will throb, the blood will leap in the veins, and the millions of living atoms of my body will vibrate in tune with the note of the harp-string that thrills at the touch of the master.

VIII

THE REALISATION OF THE INFINITE

The Upanishads say: "Man becomes true if in this life he can apprehend God; if not, it is the greatest calamity for him."

But what is the nature of this attainment of God? It is quite evident that the infinite is not like one object among many, to be definitely classified and kept among our possessions, to be used as an ally specially favouring us in our politics, warfare, money-making, or in social competitions. We cannot put our God in the same list with our summer-houses, motor-cars, or our credit at the bank, as so many people seem to want to do.

We must try to understand the true character of the desire that a man has when his soul longs for his God. Does it consist of his wish to make an addition, however valuable, to his belongings? Emphatically no! It is an endlessly wearisome task, this continual adding to our stores. In fact, when the soul seeks God she seeks her final escape from this incessant gathering and heaping and never coming to an end. It is not an additional object the she seeks, but it is the *nityo 'nityānām*, the permanent in all that is impermanent, the *rasānām rasatamah*, the highest abiding joy unifying all enjoyments. Therefore when the Upanishads teach us to realise everything in Brahma, it is not to seek something extra, not to manufacture something new.

Know everything that there is in the universe as enveloped by God.[55] *Enjoy whatever is given by him and harbour not in your mind the greed for wealth which is not your own.*[56]

When you know that whatever there is is filled by him and whatever you have is his gift, then you realise the infinite in the finite, and the giver in the gifts. Then you know that all the facts of the reality have their only meaning in the manifestation of the one truth, and all your possessions have their only significance for you, not in themselves but in the relation they establish with the infinite.

So it cannot be said that we can find Brahma as we find other objects; there is no question of searching from him in one thing in preference to another, in one place instead of somewhere else. We do not have to run to the grocer's shop for our morning light; we open our eyes and there it is; so we need only give ourselves up to find that Brahma is everywhere.

This is the reason why Buddha admonished us to free ourselves from the confinement of the life of the self. If there were nothing else to take its place more positively perfect and satisfying, then such admonition would be absolutely unmeaning. No man can seriously consider the advice, much less have any enthusiasm for it, of surrendering everything one has for gaining nothing whatever.

So our daily worship of God is not really the process of gradual acquisition of him, but the daily process of surrendering ourselves, removing all obstacles to union and extending our consciousness of him in devotion and service, in goodness and in love.

The Upanishads say: *Be lost altogether in Brahma like an arrow that has completely penetrated its target.* Thus to

55. Īçhāvāsyamdiam sarvam yat kincha jagatyānjagat.

56. Tēna tyaktēna bhunjīţhā mā gridhah kasyasviddhanam.

be conscious of being absolutely enveloped by Brahma is not an act of mere concentration of mind. It must be the aim of the whole of our life. In all our thoughts and deeds we must be conscious of the infinite. Let the realisation of this truth become easier every day of our life, that *none could live or move if the energy of the all-pervading joy did not fill the sky.*[57] In all our actions let us feel that impetus of the infinite energy and be glad.

It may be said that the infinite is beyond our attainment, so it is for us as if it were naught. Yes, if the word attainment implies any idea of possession, then it must be admitted that the infinite is unattainable. But we must keep in mind that the highest enjoyment of man is not in the having but in a getting, which is at the same time not getting. Our physical pleasures leave no margin for the unrealised. They, like the dead satellite of the earth, have but little atmosphere around them. When we take food and satisfy our hunger it is a complete act of possession. So long as the hunger is not satisfied it is a pleasure to eat. For then our enjoyment of eating touches at every point the infinite. But, when it attains completion, or in other words, when our desire for eating reaches the end of the stage of its non-realisation, it reaches the end of its pleasure. In all our intellectual pleasures the margin is broader, the limit is far off. In all our deeper love getting and non-getting run ever parallel. In one of our Vaishnava lyrics the lover says to his beloved: "I feel as if I have gazed upon the beauty of thy face from my birth, yet my eyes are hungry still: as if I have kept thee pressed to my heart for millions of years, yet my heart is not satisfied."

This makes it clear that it is really the infinite whom we seek in our pleasures. Our desire for being wealthy is not a desire for a particular sum of money but it is indefinite, and the most fleeting of our enjoyments are but the momentary

57. Ko hyevānyāt kah prānyāt yadesha ākāçha ānando na syāt.

touches of the eternal. The tragedy of human life consists in our vain attempts to stretch the limits of things which can never become unlimited,–to reach the infinite by absurdly adding to the rungs of the ladder of the finite.

It is evident from this that the real desire of our soul is to get beyond all our possessions. Surrounded by things she can touch and feel, she cries, "I am weary of getting; ah, where is he who is never to be got?"

We see everywhere in the history of man that the spirit of renunciation is the deepest reality of the human soul. When the soul says of anything, "I do not want it, for I am above it," she gives utterance to the highest truth that is in her. When a girl's life outgrows her doll, when she realises that in every respect she is more than her doll is, then she throws it away. By the very act of possession we know that we are greater than the things we possess. It is a perfect misery to be kept bound up with things lesser than ourselves. This it is that Maitreyī felt when her husband gave her his property on the eve of leaving home. She asked him, "Would these material things help one to attain the highest?"–or, in other words, "Are they more than my soul to me?" When her husband answered, "They will make you rich in worldly possessions," she said at once, "then what am I to do with these?" It is only when a man truly realises what his possessions are that he has no more illusions about them; then he knows his soul is far above these things and he becomes free from their bondage. Thus man truly realises his soul by outgrowing his possessions, and man's progress in the path of eternal life is through a series of renunciations.

That we cannot absolutely possess the infinite being is not a mere intellectual proposition. It has to be experienced, and this experience is bliss. The bird, while taking its flight in the sky, experiences at every beat of its wings that the sky is boundless, that its wings can never carry it beyond. Therein lies its joy. In the cage the sky is limited; it may be quite enough for all the purposes of the bird's life, only it is not more than is necessary. The bird cannot rejoice within the limits of the necessary. It must feel that what it has is immeasurably more than it ever can want or comprehend, and then only can it be glad.

Thus our soul must soar in the infinite, and she must feel every moment that in the sense of not being able to come to the end of her attainment is her supreme joy, her final freedom.

Man's abiding happiness is not in getting anything but in giving himself up to what is greater than himself, to ideas which are larger than his individual life, the idea of his country, of humanity, of God. They make it easier for him to part with all that he has, not expecting his life. His existence is miserable and sordid till he finds some great idea which can truly claim his all, which can release him from all attachment to his belongings. Buddha and Jesus, and all our great prophets, represent such great ideas. They hold before us opportunities for surrendering our all. When they bring forth their divine alms-bowl we feel we cannot help giving, and we find that in giving is our truest joy and liberation, for it is uniting ourselves to that extent with the infinite.

Man is not complete; he is yet to be. In what he *is* he is small, and if we could conceive him stopping there for eternity we should have an idea of the most awful hell that man can imagine. In his *to be* he is infinite, there is his heaven, his deliverance. His *is* is occupied every moment with what it can get and have done with; his *to be* is hungering for something which is more than can be got, which he never can lose because he never has possessed.

The finite pole of our existence has its place in the world of necessity. There man goes about searching for food to live, clothing to get warmth. In this region–the region of nature–it is his function to get things. The natural man is occupied with enlarging his possessions.

But this act of getting is partial. It is limited to man's necessities. We can have a thing only to the extent of our requirements, just as a vessel can contain water only to the extent of its emptiness. Our relation to food is only in feeding, our relation to a house is only in habitation. We call it a benefit when a thing is fitted only to some particular want of ours. Thus to get is always to get partially, and it never can be otherwise. So this craving for acquisition belongs to our finite self.

But that side of our existence whose direction is towards the infinite seeks not wealth, but freedom and joy. There the reign of necessity ceases, and there our function is not to get but to be. To be what? To be one with Brahma. For the region of the infinite is the region of unity. Therefore the Upanishads say: *If man apprehends God he becomes true.* Here it is becoming, it is not having more. Words do no gather bulk when you know their meaning; they become true by being one with the idea.

Though the West has accepted as its teacher him who boldly proclaimed his oneness with his Father, and who exhorted his followers to be perfect as God, it has never been reconciled to this idea of our unity with the infinite being. It condemns, as a piece of blasphemy, any implication of man's becoming God. This is certainly not the idea that Christ preached, nor perhaps the idea of the Christian mystics, but this seems to be the idea that has become popular in the Christian west.

But the highest wisdom in the East holds that it is not the function of our soul to *gain* God, to utilise him for any special material purpose. All that we can ever aspire to is to become more and more one with God. In the region of nature, which is the region of diversity, we grow by acquisition; in the spiritual world, which is the region of unity, we grow by losing ourselves, by uniting. Gaining a thing, as we have said, is by its nature partial, it is limited only to a particular want; but *being* is complete, it belongs to our wholeness, it springs not from any necessity but from our affinity with the infinite, which is the principle of perfection that we have in our soul.

Yes, we must become Brahma. We must not shrink to avow this. Our existence is meaningless if we never can expect to realise the highest perfection that there is. If we have an aim and yet can never reach it, then it is no aim at all.

But can it then be said that there is no difference between Brahma and our individual soul? Of course the difference is obvious. Call it illusion or ignorance, or whatever name you may give it, it is there. You can offer explanations but you cannot explain it away. Even illusion is true an illusion.

Brahma is Brahma, he is the infinite ideal of perfection. But we are not what we truly are; we are ever to become true, ever to become Brahma. There is the eternal play of love in the relation between this being and the becoming; and in the depth of this mystery is the source of all truth and beauty that sustains the endless march of creation.

In the music of the rushing stream sounds the joyful assurance, "I shall become the sea." It is not a vain assumption; it is true humility, for it is the truth. The river has no other alternative. On both sides of its banks it has numerous fields and forests, villages and towns; it can serve them in various ways, cleanse them and feed them, carry their produce from place to place. But it can have only partial relations with these, and however long it may linger among them it remains separate; it never can become a town or a forest.

But it can and does become the sea. The lesser moving water has its affinity with the great motionless water of the ocean. It moves through the thousand objects on its onward course, and its motion finds its finality when it reaches the sea.

The river can become the sea, but she can never make the sea part and parcel of herself. If, by some chance, she has encircled some broad sheet of water and pretends that she has made the sea a part of herself, we at once know that it is not so, that her current is still seeking rest in the great ocean to which it can never set boundaries.

In the same manner, our soul can only become Brahma as the river can become the sea. Everything else she touches at one of her points, then leaves and moves on, but she never can leave Brahma and move beyond him. Once our soul realises her ultimate object of repose in Brahma, all her movements acquire a purpose. It is this ocean of infinite rest which gives significance to endless activities. It is this perfectness of being that lends to the imperfection of becoming that quality of beauty which finds its expression in all poetry, drama and art.

There must be a complete idea that animates a poem. Every sentence of the poem touches that idea. When the reader realises that pervading idea, as he reads on, then the reading of the poem is full of joy to him. Then every part of the poem becomes radiantly significant by the light of the whole. But if the poem goes on interminably, never expressing the idea of the whole, only throwing off disconnected images, however beautiful, it becomes wearisome and unprofitable in the extreme. The progress of our soul is like a perfect poem. It has an infinite idea which once realised makes all movements full of meaning and joy. But if we detach its movements from that ultimate idea, if we do not see the infinite rest and only see the infinite motion, then existence appears to us a monstrous evil, impetuously rushing towards an unending aimlessness.

I remember in our childhood we had a teacher who used to make us learn by heart the whole book of Sanskrit grammer, which is written in symbols, without explaining their meaning to us. Day after day we went toiling on, but on towards what, we had not the least notion. So, as regards our lessons, we were in the position of the pessimist who only counts the breathless activities of the world, but cannot see the infinite repose of the perfection whence these activities are gaining their equilibrium every moment in absolute fitness and harmony. We lose all joy in thus contemplating existence, because we miss the truth. We see the gesticulations of the dancer, and we imagine these are directed by a ruthless tyranny of chance, while we are deaf to the eternal music which makes every one of these gestures inevitably spontaneous and beautiful. These motions are ever growing into that music of perfection, becoming one with it, dedicating to that melody at every step the multitudinous forms they go on creating.

And this is the truth of our soul, and this is her joy, that she must ever be growing into Brahma, that all her movements should be modulated by this ultimate idea, and all her creations should be given as offerings to the supreme spirit of perfection.

There is a remarkable saying in the Upanishads: *I think not that I know him well, or that I know him, or even that I know him not.*[58]

By the process of knowledge we can never know the infinite being. But if he is altogether beyond our reach, then he is absolutely nothing to us. The truth is that we know him not, yet we know him.

This has been explained in another saying of the Upanishads: *From Brahma words come back baffled, as well as the*

58. Nāham manye suvedeti no na vedeti vedacha.

mind, but he who knows him by the joy of him is free from all fears.[59]

Knowledge is partial, because our intellect is an instrument, it is only a part of us, it can give us information about things which can be divided and analysed, and whose properties can be classified part by part. But Brahma is perfect, and knowledge which is partial can never be a knowledge of him.

But he can be known by joy, by love. For joy is knowledge in its completeness, it is knowing by our whole being. Intellect sets us apart from the things to be known, but love knows its object by fusion. Such knowledge is immediate and admits no doubt. It is the same as knowing our own selves, only more so.

Therefore, as the Upanishads say, mind can never know Brahma, words can never describe him; he can only be known by our soul, by her joy in him, by her love. Or, in other words, we can only come into relation with him by union—union of our whole being. We must be one with our Father, we must be perfect as he is.

But how can that be? There can be no grade in infinite perfection. We cannot grow more and more into Brahma. He is the absolute one, and there can be no more or less in him.

Indeed, the realisation of the *paramātman*, the supreme soul, within our *antarātman*, our inner individual soul, is in a state of absolute completion. We cannot think of it as non-existent and depending on our limited powers for its gradual construction. If our relation with the divine were all a thing of our own making, how should we rely on it as true, and how should it lend us support?

---

59. Yato vācho nivartante aprāpya manasā saha ānandam brahmaṉo vidvān na vibheti kutaçchana.

Yes, we must know that within us we have that where space and time cease to rule and where the links of evolution are merged in unity. In that everlasting abode of the *ātaman*, the soul, the revelation of the *paramātman*, the supreme soul, is already complete. Therefore the Upanishads say: *He who knows Brahman, the true, the all-conscious, and the infinite as hidden in the depths of the soul, which is the supreme sky (the inner sky of consciousness), enjoys all objects of desire in union with the all-knowing Brahman.*[60]

The union is already accomplished. The *paramātman*, the supreme soul, has himself chosen this soul of ours as his bride and the marriage has been completed. The solemn *mantram* has been uttered: *Let thy heart be even as my heart is.*[61] There is no room in this marriage for evolution to act the part of the master of ceremonies. The *eshah*, who cannot otherwise be described than as *This*, the nameless immediate presence, is ever here in our innermost being. "This *eshah*, or *This*, is the supreme end of the other this"[62] "this *This* is the supreme treasure of the other this"[63] "this *This* is the supreme dwelling of the other this"[64] "this *This* is the supreme joy of the other this."[65] Because the marriage of supreme love has been accomplished in timeless time. And now goes on the endless *līlā*, the play of love. He who has been gained in eternity is now being pursued in time and space, in joys and sorrows, in this world and in the worlds beyond. When the soul-bride understands this well, her heart is blissful and at rest. She knows that she, like a river, has attained the ocean of her fulfilment at one end of her being, and at the other end she is ever attaining it; at one end it is

60. Satyam jñānam anantam brahma yo veda nihitam guhāyām paramo vyoman so'çnute sarvān kāmān saha brahmaṇa vipasçhite.
61. Yadetat hṛidayam mama tadastu hṛidayan tava.
62. Eshāsya paramā gatih
63. Eshāsya paramā sampat.
64. Eshāsya paramo lokah
65. Eshāsya parama ānandah

eternal rest and completion, at the other it is incessant movement and change. When she knows both ends as inseparably connected, then she knows the world as her own household by the right of knowing the master of the world as her own lord. Then all her services becomes services of love, all the troubles and tribulations of life come to her as trials triumphantly borne to prove the strength of her love, smilingly to win the wager from her lover. But so long as she remains obstinately in the dark, lifts not her veil, does not recognise her lover, and only knows the world dissociated from him, she serves as a handmaid here, where by right she might reign as a queen; she sways in doubt, and weeps in sorrow and dejection. *She passes from starvation to starvation, from trouble to trouble, and from fear to fear.*[66]

I can never forget that scrap of a song I once heard in the early dawn in the midst of the din of the crowd that had collected for a festival the night before: "Ferryman, take me across to the other shore!"

In the bustle of all our work there comes out this cry, "Take me across." The carter in India sings while driving his cart, "Take me across." The itinerant grocer deals out his goods to his customers and sings, "Take me across".

What is the meaning of this cry? We feel we have not reached our goal; and we know with all our striving and toiling we do not come to the end, we do not attain our object. Like a child dissatisfied with its dolls, our heart cries, "Not this, not this." But what is that other? Where is the further shore?

Is it something else than what we have? Is it somewhere else than where we are? Is it to take rest from all our works, to be relieved from all the responsibilities of life?

---

66. Daurbhikshāt yāti daurbhiksham kleçāt kleçam bhayāt bhayam.

No, in the very heart of our activities we are seeking for our end. We are crying for the across, even where we stand. So, while our lips utter their prayer to be carried away, our busy hands are never idle.

In truth, thou ocean of joy, this shore and the other shore are one and the same in thee. When I call this my own, the other lies estranged; and missing the sense of that completeness which is in me, my heart incessantly cries out for the other. All my this, and that other, are waiting to be completely reconciled in thy love.

This "I" of mine toils hard, day and night, for a home which it knows as its own. Alas, there will be no end of its sufferings so long as it is not able to call this home thine. Till then it will struggle on, and its heart will ever cry, "Ferryman, lead me across." When this home of mine is made thine, that very moment is it taken across, even while its old walls enclose it. This "I" is restless. It is working for a gain which can never be assimilated with its spirit, which it never can hold and retain. In its efforts to clasp in its own arms that which is for all, it hurts others and is hurt in its turn, and cries, "Lead me across". But as soon as it is able to say, "All my work is thine," everything remains the same, only it is taken across.

Where can I meet thee unless in this mine home made thine? Where can I join thee unless in this my work transformed into thy work? If I leave my home I shall not reach thy home; if I cease my work I can never join thee in thy work. For thou dwellest in me and I in thee. Thou without me or I without thee are nothing.

Therefore, in the midst of our home and our work, the prayer rises, "Lead me across!" For here rolls the sea, and even here lies the other shore waiting to be reached—yes, here is this everlasting present, not distant, not anywhere else.

Made in the USA
Monee, IL
18 October 2026

66038512R00073